DEPARTMENT OF THE ARMY TECHNICAL
DEPARTMENT OF THE AIR FORCE MANUAL

TM 9-1005-226-14
AFM50-11

OPERATION AND UNIT MAINTENANCE
CAL..22 HIGH STANDARD AUTOMATIC PISTOL (SUPERMATIC)
CAL..22 RUGER MARK I AUTOMATIC PISTOL (TARGET MODEL) (6-718 IN. BARREL)
CAL..38 SPECIAL SMITH AND WESSON REVOLVER (MASTERPIECE)
CAL..30-06 WINCHESTER RIFLE MODEL 70 (SPECIAL MATCH GRADE)
CAL..22 WINCHESTER RIFLE MODEL 52
CAL..22 REMINGTON RIFLE MODEL 40X-S1 (NATIONAL MATCH)
AND FRONT AND REAR SIGHTS

DEPARTMENTS OF THE ARMY AND THE AIR FORCE
JULY 1959

AGO 10003A-Jul

*TM 9-1005-226-14/AFM 50-11

This manual contains copyrighted material

TECHNICAL MANUAL
No. 9-1005-226-14
AIR FORCE MANUAL
No. 50-11

DEPARTMENTS OF THE ARMY
AND THE AIR FORCE

WASHINGTON 25, D. C., *20 July 1959*

CAL.22 HIGH STANDARD AUTOMATIC PISTOL (SUPERMATIC); CAL..22 RUGER MARK I AUTOMATIC PISTOL (TARGET MODEL) (607/8-IN. BARREL); CAL.38 SPECIAL SMITH AND WESSON REVOLVER K-38 (MASTERPIECE); CAL..30-06 WINCHESTER RIFLE MODEL 70 (SPECIAL MATCH GRADE); CAL.22 WINCHESTER RIFLE MODEL 52; CAL.22 REMINGTON RIFLE MODEL 40X-S1 (NATIONAL MATCH); AND FRONT AND REAR SIGHTS

			Paragraph	Page
CHAPTER	1.	INTRODUCTION		
Section	I.	General	1, 2	3
	II.	Description and data	3-5	4
CHAPTER	2.	OPERATING INSTRUCTIONS		
Section	I.	Service upon receipt of materiel	6-8	17
	II.	Controls and instruments	9-18	18
	III.	Operation under usual conditions	19-26	33
	IV.	Operation under unusual conditions	27-31	39
CHAPTER	3.	PREVENTIVE MAINTENANCE INSTRUCTIONS		
Section	I.	Parts, special tools, and equipment for operation-and preventive maintenance	32-35	41
	II.	Lubrication and preventive maintenance services	36-40	44
	III.	Troubleshooting	41-43	49
	IV.	Field stripping	44-50	51
CHAPTER	4.	MAINTENANCE INSTRUCTIONS		
Section	I.	General	51, 52	59
	II.	Parts, special tools, and equipment for maintenance	53-56	59
	III.	Inspection	57, 58	59
	IV.	Cal. 22 high-standard automatic pistol (supermatic)	59-63	62
	V.	Cal. 22 Ruger Mark I automatic pistol (target model)	64-69	68
	VI.	Cal. 38 Special, Smith and Wesson revolver K-38 (masterpiece)	70-72	71
	VII.	Cal. 22 Rifle M12 (Winchester Rifle, Model 52) (heavy barrel)	73-76	74
	VIII.	Cal. 22 Rifle M12 (Remington Rifle Model 40X-S1)	77-80	79
	IX.	Cal. 30-06 Winchester Rifle Model 70 (special match grade)	81-87	82
	X.	Sights	88, 89	87
	XI.	Final inspection	90, 91	89
CHAPTER	5.	AMMUNITION	92-94	90
CHAPTER	6.	SHIPMENT AND STORAGE	95, 96	91
APPENDIX		REFERENCES		92
INDEX				95

*This manual supersedes TM 9-2316, 20 December 1956, including 1, 15 May 1957, and so much of TB 9-2316-1, TO 1W2-1-3, 3 April 1958, including as pertains to commercial match pistols, revolvers, and rifles.

AGO 10003A

COPYRIGHT NOTICE: Copyrighted illustrations are included in this technical manual by courtesy of the following manufacturers:

Figures 1, 14, 15, 16-Hi Standard Mfg. Co.

Figures 8, 50, 63-Remington Arms Company, Inc.

Figures 28, 29, 30, 31, 33, 35, 38, 39, 64, 65—Olin Mathieson Chemical Corporation

Figure 3—Lyman Gun Sight Corporation

Figure 57—Sturm Ruger & Co., Inc.

Figure 58—Smith and Wesson, Inc.

CHAPTER 1
INTRODUCTION

Section I. GENERAL

1. Scope

a. These instructions are published for the use of personnel to whom the materiel is issued. They contain information on operation (and unit maintenance, ammunition and shipment, and limited storage of the materiel. Army publications and forms referred to herein do not apply to Air Force activities and will not be requisitioned by them.

b. The publication of this information is not to be construed as authority for the performance by maintenance personnel of those functions that have been restricted to rebuild installations. In general, the prescribed maintenance responsibilities will apply as reflected in the allocation of maintenance parts listed in the pertinent ORD 7 supply manuals. Replacement parts for pistols, revolvers, and M12 rifles are listed in SB 9-112, SB 9-125, and SB 9-135 and are procured locally.

c. The appendix contains a list of current references, including supply and technical manuals and other available publications applicable to the materiel.

d. Any errors or omissions will be recorded on DA Form 2028, and forwarded to the Commanding Officer, Raritan Arsenal, Metuchen, N.J. ATTN: ORDJR-CPRA.

e. This manual differs from TM 9-2316, 20 December 1956 as follows:

(1) Adds information on-
    Rifle, cal. .22, M12
      (Remington Model 40X-S1)
      (Winchester Model 52, Heavy Barrel)
    Sights-Lyman Rear Sight No. 525
     -Redfield Olympic No. 3
     -Front Sight Assembly

(2) Revises information on-
    Lubrication, inspection, and trouble-shooting.

(3) Deletes reference to-
    Organizational and field maintenance instructions.

2. Forms, Records, and Reports

a. General. Responsibility for the proper execution of forms, records, and reports rests upon the officers of all units maintaining this equipment. However, the value of accurate records must be fully appreciated by all persons responsible for their compilation, maintenance, and use. Records, reports, and authorized forms are normally utilized to indicate the type, quantity, and condition of materiel to be inspected to be repaired, or to be used in repair. Properly executed forms convey authorization and save as records for repair or replacement of materiel in the hands of troops and for delivery of materiel requiring further repair to ordnance shops. The forms, records, and reports establish the work required, the progress of the work within the shops, and the status of the materiel upon completion of its repair.

b. Authorized Forms. The forms generally applicable to units operating or maintaining this materiel are listed in the appendix. For a listing of all forms, refer to DA Pam 310-2. For instructions on the use of these forms, refer to FM 9-10.

c. Field Report of Accidents.

(1) *Injury to personnel or damage to materiel.* The reports necessary to comply with the requirements of the Army safety program are prescribed in detail in AR 385-40. These reports are required whenever accidents involving injury to personnel or damage to materiel occur.

AGO 10003A

(2) *Ammunition.* Whenever an accident or malfunction involving the use of ammunition occurs, firing of the lot which malfunctions will be immediately discontinued. In addition to any applicable reports required in (1) above, details of the accident or malfunction will be reported as prescribed in AR 700-1300-8.

d. Report of Unsatisfactory Equipment or Materials. Any deficiencies detected in the equipment covered herein which occur under circumstances indicated in AR 700-38, should be immediately reported in accordance with the applicable instructions in cited regulation.

Section II. DESCRIPTION AND DATA

3. Description

a. Cal..22 High Standard Automatic Pistol Supermatic). The supermatic pistol (figs. 1 and 2) is a 10-shot magazine-loaded cal..22 weapon, chambered for the cal..22 long rifle cartridge only. The rear sight has a precision click adjustment for windage and elevation. The front sight is of the inclined ramp type. The 6 ¾ -inch long barrel has ports near its muzzle to stabilize it against muzzle jump. Weights of 2 to 5 ounces may be added to a dovetailed slot in the barrel to give balance to the pistol. A positive lock safety is provided which locks the sear in the safe position. A slide lock is used to hold the slide assembly in the open position. It automatically holds the slide open after firing the last round in the magazine. Takedown of the barrel and the slide assembly is easily accomplished by depressing a barrel plunger cam. The magazine assembly is released by means of the magazine catch. The trigger is of the serrated type for nonslip action. The grips are diamond checkered solid

b. Cal..22 Ruger Mark I Automatic Pistol (Target Model) (6 7/8 - In. Barrel). The Ruger pistol mark I (figs. 3 and 4) is a 9-shot magazine-loaded cal..22 weapon, chambered for the cal..22 long rifle cartridge only. The "micro" rear sight is attached to the receiver and does not move with the recoil action of the weapon. The sight has precision click adjustment for windage and elevation. The front sight is a patridge style with a 0.125-inch wide blade. The bolt assembly which slides inside the receiver has serrated lugs used in initially cocking the weapon. A positive lock safety lever is provided which locks the sear in the safe position. It also can be used to lock the bolt in the rear position for chamber inspection. Takedown is easily accomplished by removing the mainspring housing assembly and sliding the barrel and receiver from the frame group. The trigger of the serrated type for nonslip action. The rips are butaprene hard black gloss rubber with diamond checkering.

c. Cal..38 Special, Smith and Wesson Revolver K-38 (Masterpiece). The cal..38 revolver K-38 (masterpiece) (figs. 5 and 6) is a 6-shot breech-loading hand weapon. It has a solid frame, a swing out cylinder with six chambers, and a manual ejector. The cylinder, mounted on a yoke assembled to the front of the frame, swings out when released by the thumbpiece. The cylinder is unloaded by pressure on the ejector rod which passes down the central axis of the cylinder. Spring loading returns the ejector rod to its original position. This revolver is a selective-double-action type or single-action type. There is a built-in safety which prevents firing except by pull on the trigger. The front sight is /8 or 0o-inch wide plain patridge style. The rear sight has micrometer click adjustments for windage and elevation. The grips are walnut wood with diamond checkering. The hammer spur and trigger are knurled.

d. Cal..22 Rifle M12 (Winchester Model 52, Heavy Barrel). The cal..22 rifle M12 designates commercial rifles classified for match competition for armed services and includes the weapons described in (1) and (2) below.

(1) The cal..22 rifle (Winchester Model 52, heavy barrel) (fig. 7) is a bolt-action 5-shot magazine-loaded repeating rifle, chambered for the long rifle cal..22 cartridge only. The rear sight may be a Lyman No. 525 or Redfield Olympic

AGO 10003A

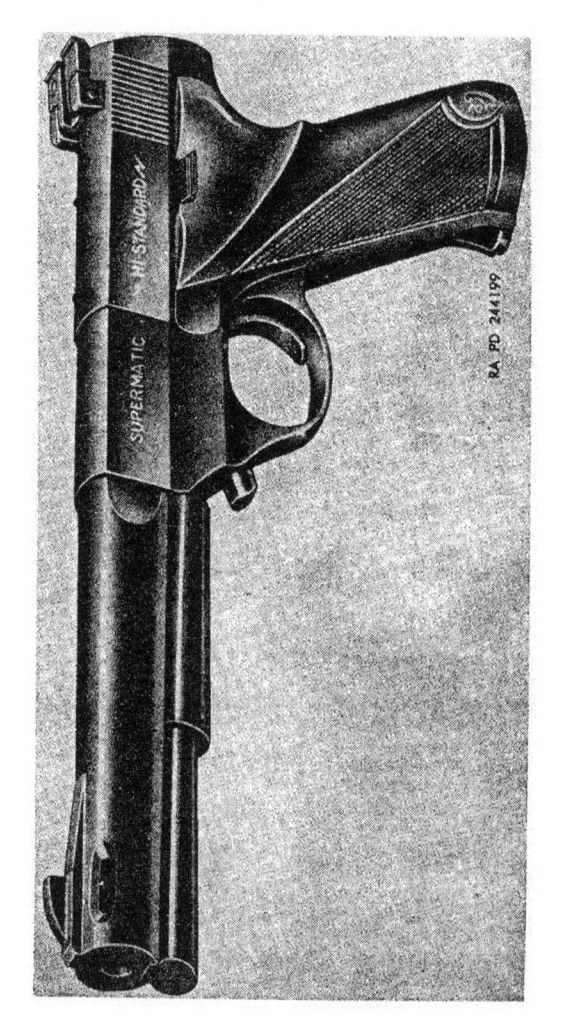

Figure 1. Cal. .22 high standard automatic pistol (supermatic) three-quarter left-front view.

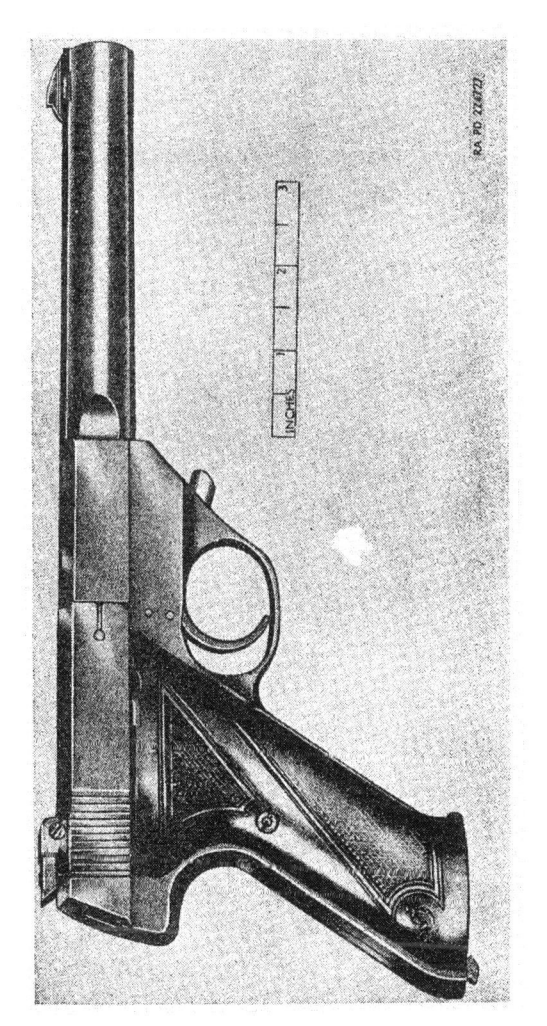

Figure 2. Cal. .22 high standard automatic pistol (supermatic) three-quarter right-rear view.

Figure 3. Cal. .22 Ruger Mark I automatic pistol (target model) (6 7/8-in. barrel) three-quarter left-rear view.

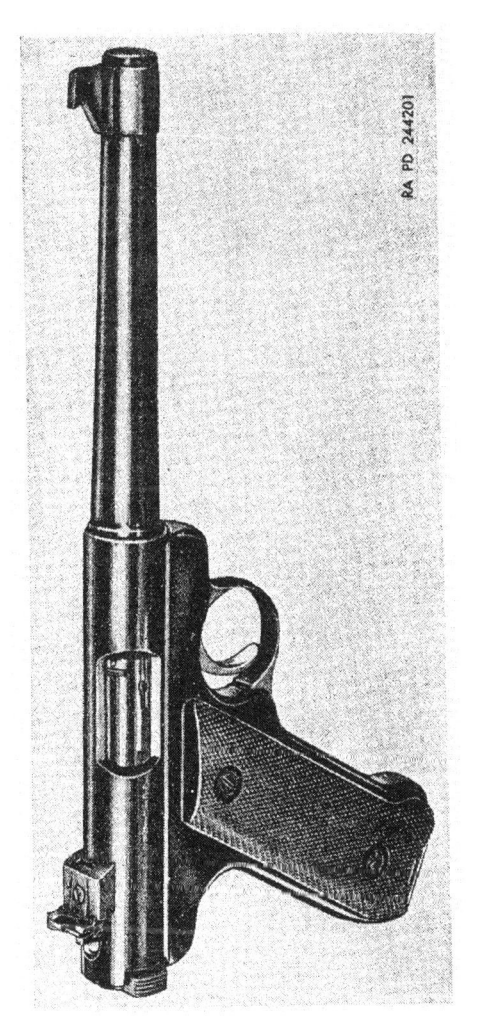

Figure 4. Cal. 22 Ruger Mark I automatic pistol (target model) three-quarter right-front view.

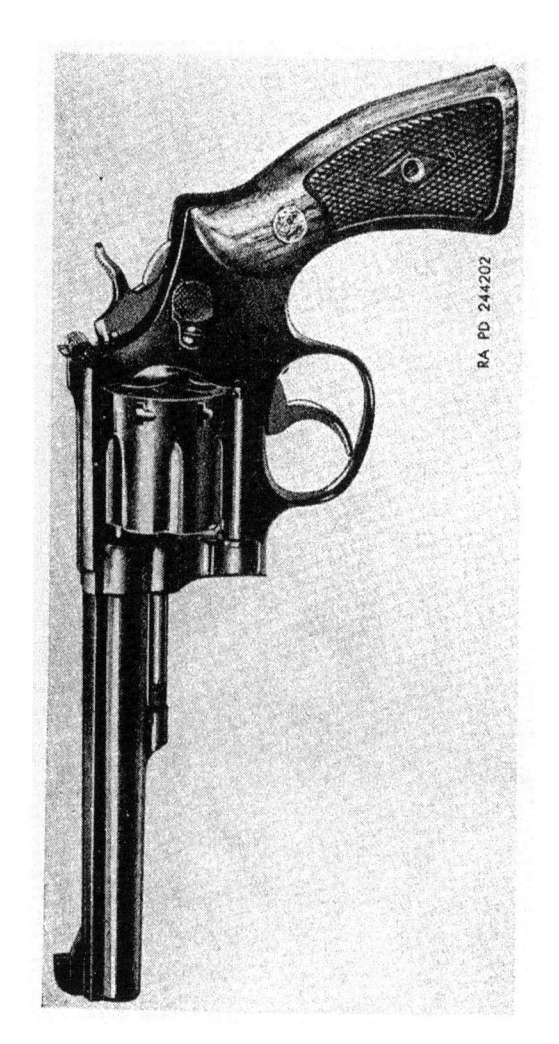

Figure 5. Cal..38 Special Smith and Wesson revolver K-38 (masterpiece) three-quarter left-rear view.

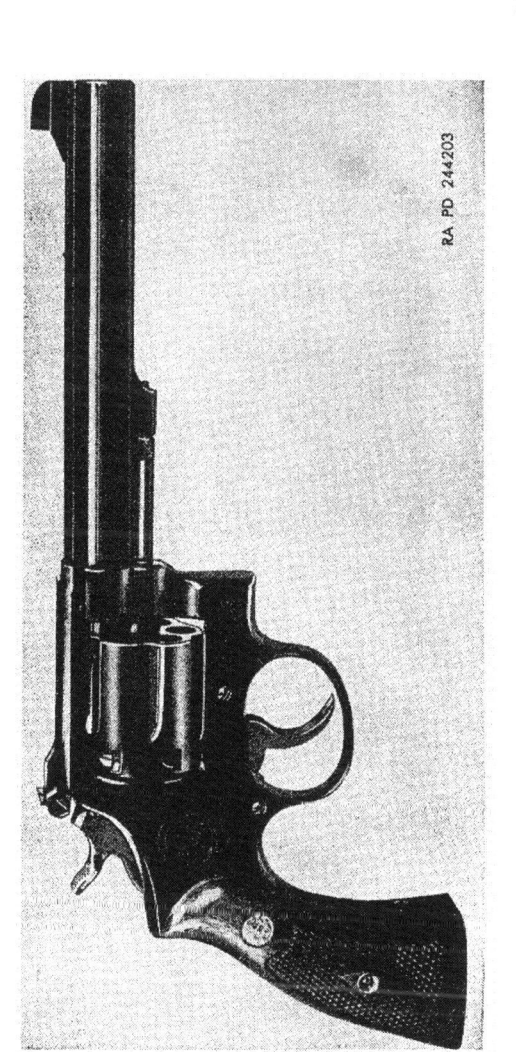

Figure 6. Cal. 38 Special Smith and Wesson revolver K-38 (masterpiece) three-quarter right-front view.

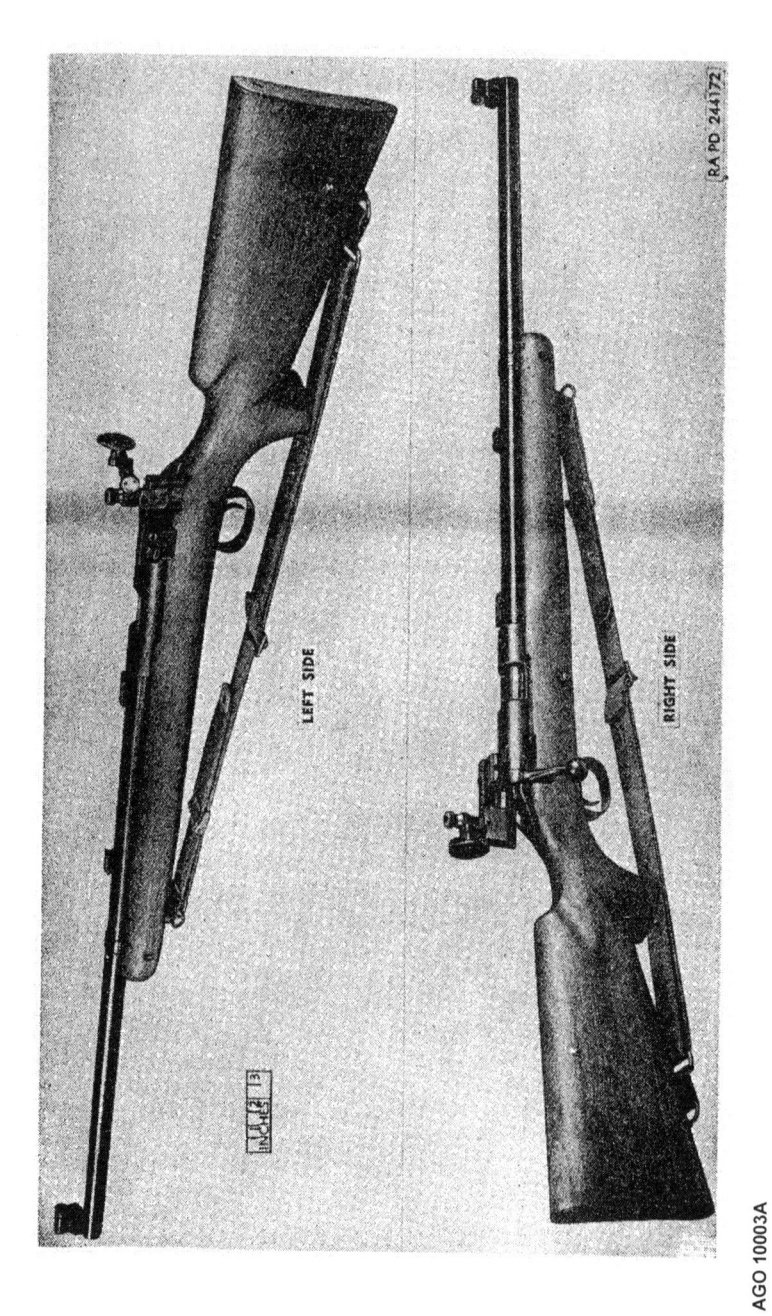

Figure 7. Cal. .22 rifle M12 (Winchester model 52, heavy barrel) left and right sides.

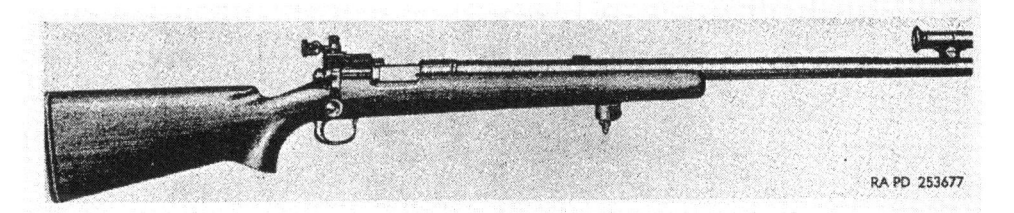

Figure 8. Cal..22 Rifle M12 (Remington model 40X-S1).

receiver sight or a telescope. The front sight may be a Lyman No. 77 or Redfield Olympic with interchangeable inserts. The safety lock is located at the front of the bolt locking handle.

(2) The cal..22 rifle M12 (Remington Model 40X-S1) (fig. 8) is a bolt-action single-shot weapon with loading platform, and is chambered for the 22 long rifle cartridge only. The rear sight is a Redfield Olympic receiver sight. The front sight is a Redfield Olympic with 10 interchangeable inserts. Provisions for mounting a telescope are provided. The safety lock is located at the top rear of the bolt.

e. Cal..30-06 Winchester Rifle Model 70 (Special Match Grade). The Winchester rifle Model 70 (fig. 9) is a bolt-action 5-shot magazine loaded repeating weapon. The rear sight is a Lyman No. 48WH sight which has click sight adjustments for windage and elevation. The sight can easily be removed from the sight base by loosening the lock bolt knob. The front sight is a Lyman No. 77 which is a hooded detachable sight with nine interchangeable inserts. Provisions for mounting a telescope are provided. The safety lock is located at the top rear of the bolt. The bolt stop at rear of receiver holds the bolt in the receiver. The magazine located in the receiver is nonprotruding and has a hinged floor plate. The plate is released by the magazine cover catch in the guard bow. The stock is of walnut wood with a checkered steel butt plate. A detachable 1l/4-inch leather strap sling is provided.

4. Name and Data Plates

a. Cal..22 High-Standard Automatic Pistol Supermatic).

(1) The word "Supermatic" appears on the left-hand side of the pistol on the barrel trunnion.

(2) The word "Hi-Standard" appears at the left side of the slide. The model number appears on the right side of the slide assembly with the serial number. On the flat on the right side of the barrel, the word "High-Standard Mfg. Corp., Hamden, Conn., U.S.A., .22 long rifle" appears. The frame has the serial number on the left-rear top which can be seen when slide is removed. The magazine has the words "Hi-Standard" on the floor plate.

b. Cal..22 Ruger Mark I Automatic Pistol (Target Model) (6 7/8 In. Barrel). The Ruger pistol has the manufacturer's name and address on the right side of the receiver (fig. 10) and the serial number ahead of the ejection chamber (fig. 10). The right side of the receiver contains the name and model of the pistol (fig. 11). The grips have the manufacturer's medallion on them.

c. Cal..38 Special, Smith and Wesson Revolver K-38 (Masterpiece).

(1) The trade-mark appears on the side plate (fig. 12). The left side of the frame has U.S. marking. On the right side of the frame, the manufacturer's name and address are found (fig. 12). The barrel has "Smith and Wesson" stamped on the left side and "S&W 38 Special" stamped on the right side.

(2) The serial number appears on the underside of the grip and underside of the barrel (fig. 13). The grips have the manufacturer's medallion engraved in the wood.

AGO 10003A

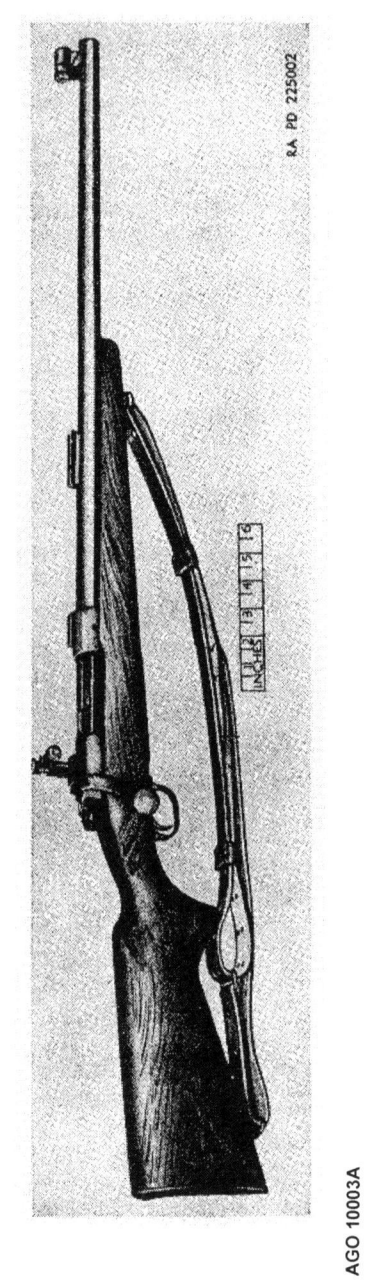

Figure 9. Cal. .30-06 Winchester rifle model 70 (special match grade).

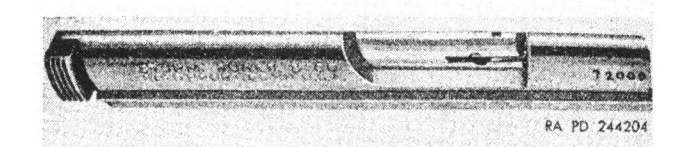

Figure 10. Name and serial plate (Ruger).

Figure 11. Nameplate (Ruger).

Figure 12. Nameplate (Smith and Wesson).

Figure 13. Serial number (Smith and Wesson).

AGO 10003A

d. *Cal..22 Rifle M12 (Winchester Model 52, Heavy Barrel).*
  (1) The trade mark appears on the receiver. The barrel is inscribed "Winchester Model 52, Caliber .22 Long Rifle."
  (2) The serial number appears on the receiver.

  e. *Cal..22 Rifle M12 (Remington Model 40X-S1).*
  (1) The left side of the receiver is inscribed "Remington Model 40-X, cal. .22 long rifle."
  (2) The receiver is marked with manufacturer's serial number and proofmark.

  f. *Cal..30-06 Winchester Rifle Model 70 (Special Match Grade).*
  (1) The barrel is marked with model numbers, manufacturer's trademark, caliber, and proofmark.
  (2) The receiver is marked with manufacturer's trademark, serial number, and proofmark.
  (3) The bolt has the serial number duplicated with an electric pencil.

5. **Tabulated Data**
  a. *Cal..22 High-Standard Automatic Pistol (Supermatic).*
Weight, with 6⅝-inch barrel ------ 42 oz
Caliber of bore --------------------- 0.22 in.
Rifling:
  Number of grooves ------ 6
  Right-hand twist (one 16 in. turn in) -----------------
Magazine capacity ---------------- 10 cart
Trigger pull 2 ------------------------- 3 lb
Rear sight -------------------------- micrometer click sight
Front sight -------------------------- adjustable ramp

  b. *Cal..22 Ruger Mark I Automatic Pistol (Target Model) (6 7/8-In. Barrel).*
Weight ------------------------------ 42 oz
Caliber of bore --------------------- 0.22 in.
Barrel length ------------------------ 6 7/8 in.
Overall length ---------------------- 10 7/8 in.
Rifling:
  Number of grooves ------ 6
  Twist (one turn in) -------- 14 in.
Magazine capacity ---------------- 9 cart.
Trigger pull ------------------------- 2 ¼ - 3 1/4 lb
Rear sight -------------------------- micrometer click sight
Front sight -------------------------- patridge style
  Sight radius   9 3/8 in.

  c. *Cal..38 Special, Smith and Wesson Revolver K48 (Masterpiece).*
Weight (loaded) -------------------- 38.5 oz
Caliber of bore --------------------- 0.3465 in.
Barrel length ----------------------- 6 in.
Overall length ---------------------- 11 1/8 in.
Rifling:
  Number of grooves ----- 5
  Right-hand twist --------- 18 3/4 in. (one turn in).
Number of cylinder chambers -- 6
Trigger pull:
  Single action -------------- 2 ½ to 3 1/2 lb
  Double action ------------ 12 to 14 lb
Rear sight --------------------------- micrometer click sight
Front sight -------------------------- 1/8- or 1/10-in. plain patridge.

  d. *Cal..22 Rifle M12 (Winchester Model 52, Heavy Barrel)*
Weight ------------------------------ 11 lb, 10 oz
Caliber of bore --------------------- 0.22 in.
Barrel length ----------------------- 27.50 in.
Overall length ---------------------- 45.8 in.
Rifling length ----------------------- 26.75 in.
Number of lands and grooves -- 6
Twist Right hand ------------------ one turn in 16 in.
Magazine capacity ---------------- 5 cart.
Sight radius ------------------------ 33.8 in.
Height of front sight from 1.189 in.
  center of bore.
Loading device -------------------- magazine
Ammunition ------------------------ cartridge, cal..22, ball long rifle. (See chapter 4 for complete ammunition data.)

  Performance
Approximate range for 1,500 yd
  cartridge.
Normal pressure ------------------ 20,000 lb per sq. in.
Muzzle velocity -------------------- 1,100 ft per see

  e. *Cal..22 Rifle M12 (Remington, M40X-S1).*
  (1) *General.*
Weight ------------------------ 10 lb, 12 oz
Overall length ------------- 46 3/4 in.
Barrel length -------------- 28 in.
Number of lands and --- 6
  grooves.
Twist of rifling right ----- one turn in 16 in. hand.
Single shot ---------------- hand loaded (one cartridge).
Ammunition -------------- cartridge, cal..22 ball, long rifle. (See chapter 5 for complete ammunition data.)

15

(2) Performance.
   Approximate maximum 1,500 yd
   range for cartridge.
   Normal pressure --------- 20,000 lb per sq in.
   Muzzle velocity ----------- 1,100 ft per sec
   f. Cal..30-06 Winchester Rifle, Model 70 (Special Match Grade).
Weight ------------------------------- 9 1/2 lb
caliber of bore ---------------------- 0.300 in.
Barrel length ----------------------- 24 in.
Overall length ---------------------- 44 3/8in.
Rifling
   Number of grooves ----- 4
   Twist (one turn in) ------- 10 in.
Magazine capacity---------------- 5 cart.
Trigger pull ------------------------- 4 to 5 1/2 lb
Front sight ------------------------- Lyman No. 77
Rear sight ------------------------- Lyman No. 48WH

AGO 10008A

CHAPTER 2
OPERATING INSTRUCTIONS

Section I. SERVICE UPON RECEIPT OF MATERIEL

6. General

a. When new or reconditioned materiel is first received by the using organization, it is necessary for the unit gunsmith to determine whether the materiel is complete and has been properly prepared for service by the supplying organization.

b. A record should be made of any missing parts and of any malfunctions.

c. The materiel should be cleaned and prepared for service in accordance with the instructions given in paragraphs 7 and 8.

7. New Materiel

a. Unpack weapon from its shipping container.

b. Remove any preservative compound (par. 38).

c. Field strip the weapon, as required (pars. 44 through 50).

d. Thoroughly clean the weapon by wiping any oil from exposed parts. Check parts for cracks or other visual defects.

e. Clean the bore as described in paragraph 38.

f. Further check the weapons as outlined in (1) through (5) below.

　(1) *High standard automatic pistol.* Check functioning of the magazine catch (par. 10a), slide lock lever (par. 10e), and safety lever (par. 10b). Operate the slide assembly (par. 10g).

　(2) *Ruger Mark I automatic pistol.* Check functioning of the safety catch (par.11a), bolt assembly (par. 11c), and magazine catch (par. 11b). Cock the bolt (par. 11c).

　(3) *Smith and Wesson revolver special K38.* Operate the thumb piece (par. 0003A 12a) and swing the cylinder to the open position. Depress extractor rod (par. 12b) and check if spring loading returns it to position. Check functioning of the hammer (par. 12c) and trigger (par. 12f).

　(4) *Winchester rifle Model 70.*
　　(a) Check front sight for proper insert (par. 17b) and rear sight for functioning (par. 16).
　　(b) New rifles have bolts packaged separately from the rifles. Check serial number of bolt against serial number of receiver.
　　(c) Check functioning of the safety lock (par. 15e), bolt handle (par. 15a), magazine cover catch (par. 15d), and magazine.
　　(d) Cock the bolt and dry fire the weapon.

　(5) *Cal..22 rifles M12.*
　　(a) Check front sight for proper insert (par. 17) and receiver extension rear sight for functioning (par. 18).
　　(b) Check functioning of safety lever (pars. 13 and 14), bolt handle (pars. 13 and 14), and magazine (par. 13b). The Remington rifle M40X-S1 has no magazine.

g. Lubricate the weapon (par. 36).

h. Check spare parts and accessories with the appropriate Department of the Army publication.

8. Used Materiel

Used materiel requires the same inspection and service prescribed for new materiel (par. 7). In addition, check all components for signs of wear and corrosion. Check for missing parts and replace as required.

Section II. CONTROLS AND INSTRUMENTS

9. General

This section describes, locates, and illustrates all controls and instruments provided for the materiel.

10. Cal..22 High-Standard Automatic Pistol (Supermatic) *a. Magazine Catch.*

(1) The magazine catch is located on the lower-rear portion of the grip frame. It is serrated for nonslip action.

(2) To release the magazine assembly, depress the catch rearward. Spring action will return the catch to its original position.

b. Safety Lever.

(1) The safety lever (fig. 14)is located at top left side of the frame. It acts on the sear to prevent release of the hammer.

(2) Move safety lever up to put pistol on SAFE position. Move safety lever downward to put pistol in FIRE position.

(3) The safety lever in SAFE position locks the slide assembly (fig. 15) in place.

c. Magazine Assembly. The magazine assembly (fig. 16) has a 10-cartridge capacity. The spring-loaded magazine follower is depressed by means of the magazine button in order to insert a cartridge. The cartridges are inserted, rim end first, through the front of the magazine lips (fig. 16).

d. Barrel Weights.

(1) The balance of the pistol may be changed by adding weights (fig. 46) to the bottom of the barrel assembly. A 2- or 3-ounce weight or both may be added to a dovetail slot at the bottom of the barrel. This gives

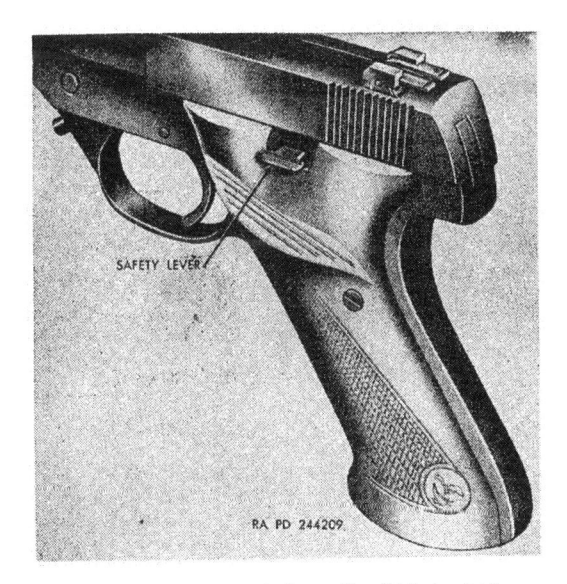

Figure 14. Safety lever in fire position (high standard).

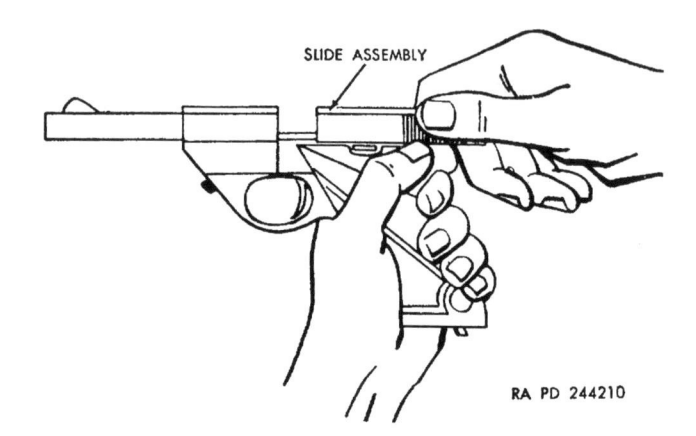

Figure 15. Retracting the slide assembly (high standard).

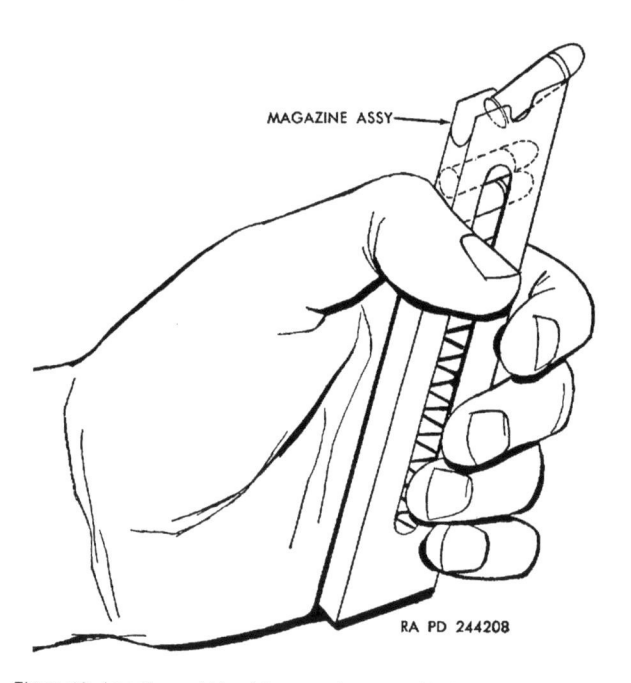

Figure 16. Inserting cartridge into magazine assembly (high standard).

the pistol a range of weights of 43 to 48 ounces.
  (2) To add weights, loosen the filler plate screws and slide the filler plate from the front of the barrel. Insert weight or weights in the dovetail slot and tighten the barrel weight screws.
e. *Slide Lock Lever.*
  (1) The slide lock lever (X, fig. 54) is located on the upper right part of the grip frame. It locks the slide in the rearward position. After the last cartridge has been fired from the magazine, the slide will be automatically held in rearward position by the slide lock lever.
  (2) To hold slide assembly in rearward position, push slide lock lever rearward.
  (3) To release slide assembly, push down on the slide lock lever.
f. *Barrel Plunger.*
  (1) The barrel plunger is located beneath the trigger guard. Cam action of the plunger and the barrel lock holds the barrel assembly.
  (2) To release the barrel assembly, depress the plunger. Spring action will return the plunger to its original position.
g. *Adjustable Rear Sight Assembly.*
  Note. **The key letters shown below in parentheses refer to figure 52.**
  (1) *General.* The adjustable rear sight assembly (B) fits in a dovetail on the slide assembly (A). The rear sight leaf (B4) is raised or lowered by the rear sight elevation screw (B3). The leaf can be adjusted for windage by the rear sight windage screw (B2). The rear sight spring (B5) keeps the leaf under spring tension and provides the click action for the windage screw.
  (2) *Rear sight elevation screw* (B3). Turning the screw clockwise raises the point of impact of the bullet. Four clicks or one turn of screw will move the impact 0.892 inch at a range of 25 feet.
  (3) *Rear sight windage screw* (B2). Turning windage screw clockwise will move 20 the point of impact of the bullet to the left. One click or one-quarter turn of the screw will move the impact 0.145 inch at a range of 25 feet.
h. *Slide Assembly.*
  (1) The slide assembly (fig. 15) is located to the rear of the barrel assembly. It contains the firing pin group, driving spring group, and extractor group.
  (2) Drawing back on the slide assembly cocks the hammer.
  (3) A cartridge will be stripped from the magazine assembly and chambered when the slide assembly is allowed to go into battery under the tension of the driving spring.

11. **Cal..22 Ruger Mark I Automatic Pistol (Target Model (6 7/8-In. Barrel)**
  a. *Safety Catch.*
    (1) The safety catch (fig. 17) is located on the upper left side of the grip frame behind the grip. S and F markings indicate the safe. and fire positions. A spring loaded detent ball holds the safety catch in place on the frame. The safety catch action is positive to hold the hammer from being released by trigger action.
    (2) Pressing the safety catch up with the left thumb puts the pistol on safe. Pressing the safety catch down with the left thumb allows the pistol to be fired.
    (3) The bolt assembly will be held in the cocked position (fig. 17) by pressing the safety into the upward position. This locks the safety into a notch on the bolt.
  b. *Magazine Catch.*
    (1) The magazine catch is located at the bottom of the grip frame (fig. 19). It is serrated for nonslip action.
    (2) Pressing the magazine catch rearward releases the magazine assembly. The catch is spring loaded for return to its original position.
  c. *Bolt Assembly.*
    (1) The bolt assembly is cylindrically shaped. It reciprocates in a well in

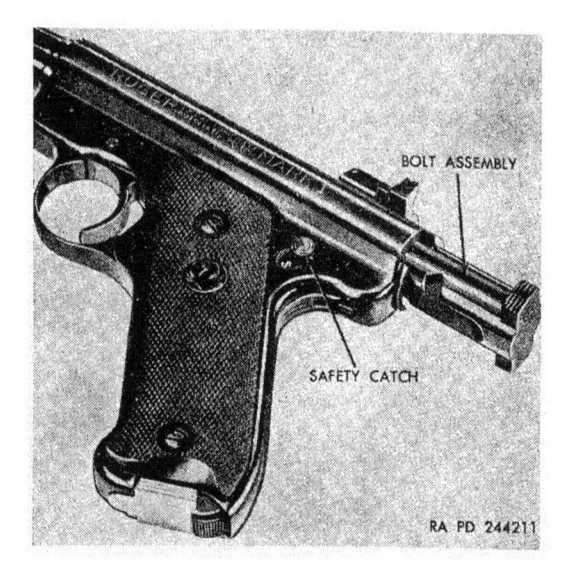

Figure 17. Bolt assembly cocked and safety catch in safe position (Ruger).

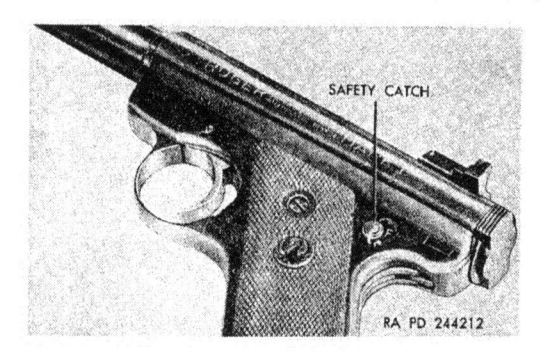

Figure 18. Safety catch in "fire" position (Ruger).

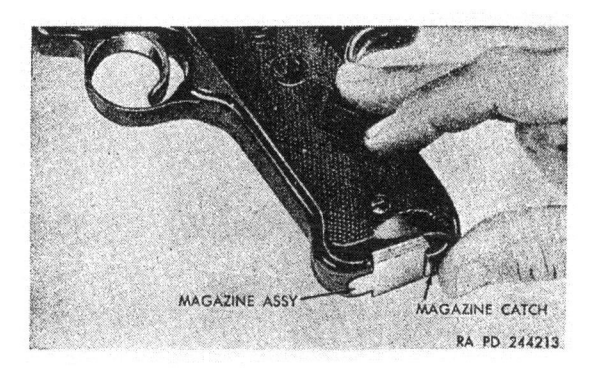

Figure 19. Removing or installing magazine assembly (Ruger).

the receiver. The extractor, located in a slot at the front of the bolt, is held in place on the bolt by a lug on the spring-loaded extractor plunger. The recoil guide spring assembly which returns the bolt to battery is held at one end by the bolt stop pivot (fig. 47) and at the firing pin end by a slot in the bolt. The recoil spring support (fig. 55) also serves as a support for the firing pin.

(2) To load the first cartridge into the chamber, insert loaded magazine, and pull back on the serrated lugs on the rear of the bolt assembly (fig. 17) until the bolt is in rear position. The recoil guide spring assembly will return the bolt to battery.

(3) To inspect barrel chamber, withdraw the bolt as described in b above and, while holding in this position, press safety catch upward as described in a above.

d. *Micro Rear Sight.*
  (1) *General.* The micro rear sight fits into a dovetail slot at the rear of the receiver. The micro rear sight hinge (fig. 21) is pivoted at the front of the rear sight base. The hinge is held at a set elevation by two rear sight hinge springs and a hinge steadying spring.
  The micro rear sight leaf (fig. 20) slides in a slot in the hinge. It is spring 22 loaded and can be moved by the rear sight windage screw. The leaf has a rectangular notch for an aperture.
  (2) *Rear sight elevation screw.*
    (a) The rear sight elevation screw (fig. 20) is located at the rear of the receiver in front of the micro sight leaf. The serrated head of the screw rests against a spring-loaded ball to give positive positioning. Spring loading of the click ball is obtained from the micro rear sight hinge springs (fig. 21) which are eccentric to the elevation screw.
    (b) The micro rear sight hinge (fig. 21) has elevation index (fig. 20) marks engraved at 45-degree intervals corresponding to each click. Turning the elevation screw clockwise lowers the impact of the bullet 1/2 inch at a 15-yard range.
  (3) *Rear sight windage screw.*
    (a) The rear sight windage screw (fig. 20) is located at the right side of the receiver under the micro sight leaf. The screw has a cup end which rests against a cone shape on the leaf which makes the click sounds. The micro sight leaf is spring loaded to provide for movement of the leaf. This spring also acts on the click cone.

22

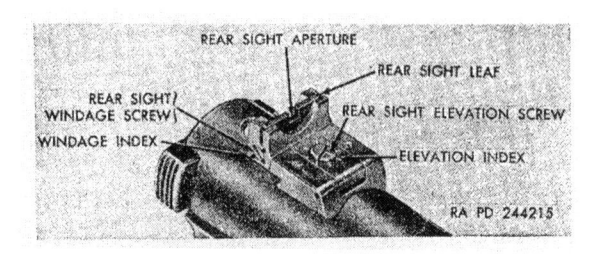

Figure 20. Micro rear sight (Ruger).

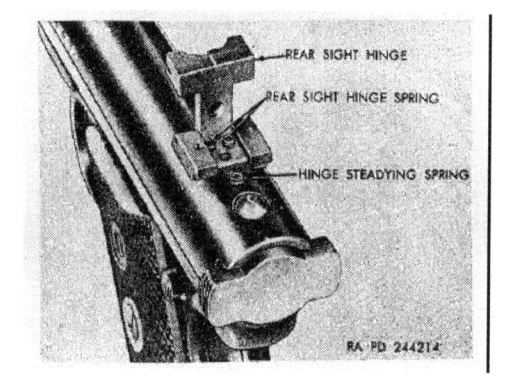

Figure 21. Micro rear sight with elevation screw removed (Ruger).

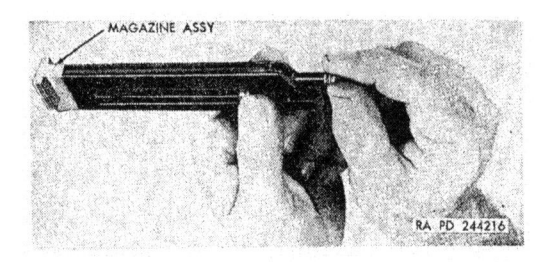

Figure 22. Loading a cartridge into magazine assembly.

(b) The micro rear sight base has windage index marks (fig. 20) engraved at 90-degree intervals corresponding to one click. Turning the windage screw clockwise, one click, moves the impact of the bullet 1/2 inch to the left at a 15-yard range.

  e. *Magazine Assembly.* The magazine assembly (fig. 22) has a 9-cartridge capacity. It fits into a well at the bottom of the grip. The magazine follower (fig. 56) is made of cast aluminum.

12. **Cal..38 Special, Smith and Wesson Revolver K-38 (Masterpiece)**
  a. *Thumb piece.*
    (1) The thumb piece (fig. 23) is located on the left side of the revolver above the stock. It is knurled and shaped to fit the thumb.
    (2) Pressing the thumb piece forward depresses the bolt plunger. This depresses the center rod which in turn depresses the locking bolt, thus releasing the cylinder and yoke group. Spring loading returns the thumb piece to its original position.
  b. *Extractor Rod.*
    (1) The extractor rod (fig. 24) is located in the center of the cylinder and yoke group and is knurled at the forward end.
    (2) After releasing the cylinder, depressing the rod rearward extracts empty shells or cartridges. The extractor rod will return to its normal position, due to spring loading.
  c. *Hammer.*
    (1) The hammer (fig. 25) is located at the rear of the frame above the stock. It is knurled and shaped to fit the thumb.
    (2) Depress the hammer fully downward and to the rear, to cock the revolver for single action firing.
    (3) Depressing the hammer to one-quarter full cock allows the cylinder to be rotated.

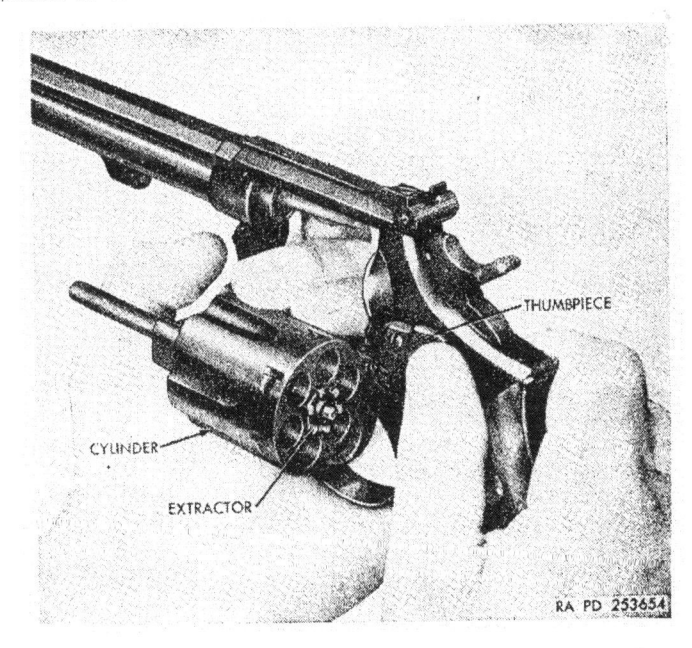

Figure 23. Pushing thumb piece to release cylinder (Smith and Wesson)

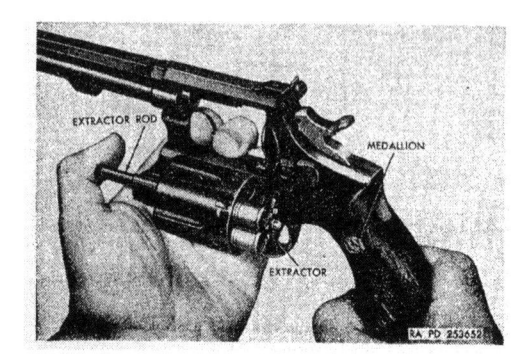

Figure 24. Unloading empty cartridge case from cylinder by depressing extractor rod (Smith and Wesson).

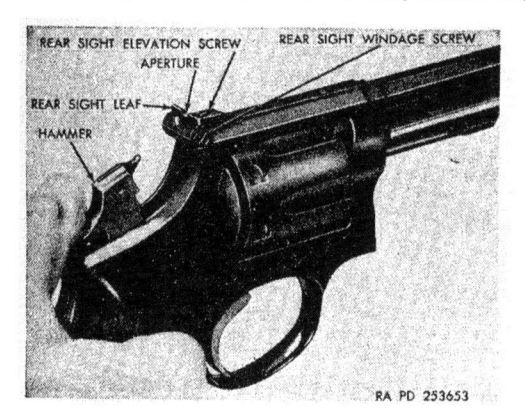

Figure 25. Cocking hammer to single action position (Smith and Wesson).

(4) To lower cocked hammer on a loaded chamber without firing, draw the hammer slightly to the rear with the thumb. Press the trigger to disengage it from the hammer. Let hammer down slowly a short distance. Release trigger and lower hammer carefully as far as it will go.

d. *Cylinder and Yoke.* The cylinder (fig. 23) and yoke swing out to the left side of the revolver for loading and ejecting. The cylinder rotates counterclockwise one-sixth revolution during the cocking of the hammer. The spring-loaded cylinder stop projects through a slot in the frame and into a rectangular cut in the cylinder. This holds the cartridge chamber aligned with the barrel and steady, during firing.

e. *Safety Device.* The safety device is internally

built into the revolver. A projection on the lower end of the hammer, resting against the upper surface of the rebound slide, prevents the hammer from moving forward to strike the primer, except when the trigger is all the way to the rear. An accidental blow on the hammer cannot cause the revolver to fire.

   f. *Trigger.*
      (1) For double action firing, apply pressure to the trigger.
      (2) For firing single action, apply pressure to the trigger after the hammer has been cocked as described in c above.

   g. *Rear Sight Elevation Screw (fig. 25).*
      (1) The rear sight elevation screw is located directly in front of the sight leaf on the rear of the frame.
      (2) Turning the screw clockwise one click, moves point of bullet impact downward 1/2 inch at a range of 25 yards.

   h. *Rear Sight Windage Screw (fig. 25).*
      (1) The rear sight windage screw is located on the right side of the revolver beneath the sight leaf. A center index mark on the sight base locates the center position of the leaf.
      (2) Turning the screw clockwise one click, moves point of bullet impact 1/2 inch to the left for a range of 25 yards.

13. Cal..22 Rifle M12 (Winchester Rifle Model 52, Heavy Barrel)

   a. *Breech Bolt Handle (fig. 26).*
      (1) The breech bolt handle is located at the rear right side of the bolt assembly.
      (2) Lifting up the bolt handle cocks the firing pin.
      (3) Pulling the bolt handle and bolt assembly completely rearward extracts and ejects a cartridge.
      (4) Pushing forward on the bolt handle seats another cartridge from the magazine into the chamber.
      (5) Turning the bolt handle down will lock the breech ready for firing.

   b. *Magazine.* The magazine is located in the opening in the bottom of the stock just forward of the trigger. In this position, its follower forces each new cartridge into the path of the breech bolt assembly. The magazine consists of the magazine tube, the follower, the spring and the base. A magazine release plunger is located on the right side of the stock.

   c. *Safety Lever.*
      (1) *General.* The safety lever (fig. 26) is located at the front of the bolt handle and operates on a horizontal plane. It is shaped to fit the thumb.
      (2) *Safe.* When the safety lever lock is at the rear of its slot, both the firing pin and bolt are positively locked.
      (3) *Fire.* When the safety lever is at the front of its slot, the rifle is ready to be fired.

14. Cal..22 Rifle M12 (Remington Model 40OXS1)

   a. *Bolt Handle* (fig. 27). Refer to paragraph 13a. After inserting a cartridge by hand, pushing forward on the bolt handle seats the cartridge in the chamber.

   b. *Bolt Assembly.*
      (1) safety forward to the FIRE position and press up on the bolt stop release located just forward of the trigger.
      (2) Rotate bolt handle up and away from right side of receiver, and pull the bolt out of the rear of the receiver.

   c. *Magazine.* The Remington rifle Model 40X-S1 is a single-shot weapon and has no magazine.

   d. *Safety (fig. 27).*
      (1) *General.* The safety is to the rear of the bolt on the right side of the receiver.
      (2) *Safe.* The thumb piece of the safety is to the rear. With the safety in the SAFE position, the bolt handle only is located in the down position.
      (3) *Fire.* When the safety is in the FIRE position, the bolt handle can be raised to unlock the bolt and open the action for loading the weapon. Operation of the trigger will release the firing pin and fire the loaded weapon.

   e. *Trigger.* The trigger (fig. 27) is located in the bottom of the stock immediately below the bolt handle

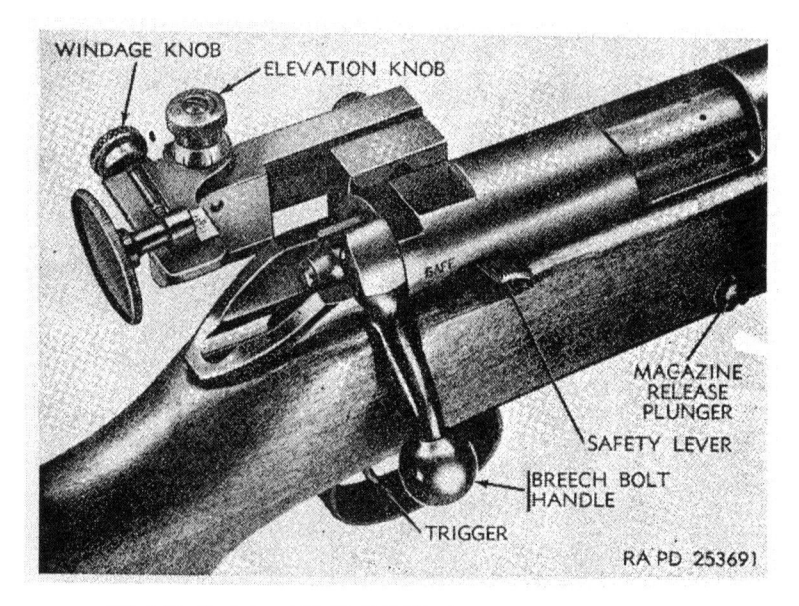

Figure 26. Controls cal..22 rifle M12 (Winchester model 52, heavy barrel).

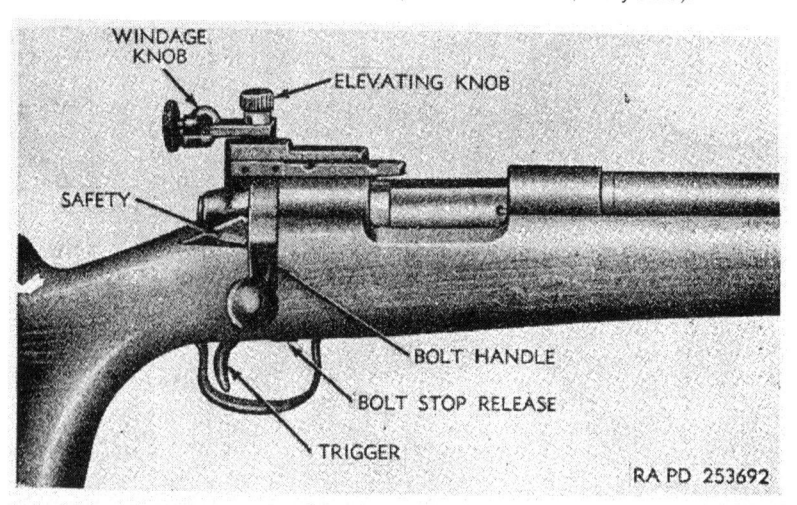

Figure 27. Controls cal..22 rifle M12 (Remington model 40X-S1).

and is operated by squeezing to the rear against the tension of the trigger spring. The squeezing of the trigger releases the firing pin permitting the sharp end of the pin to strike to rim of the cartridge.

15. Cal 30-06 Winchester Rifle Model 70 (Special Match Grade)

a. Bolt Handle (fig. 27).
 (1) The bolt handle is located at the rear right side of the bolt assembly.
 (2) Lifting up on the bolt handle cocks the firing pin.
 (3) Pulling the bolt handle and bolt assembly completely rearward extracts and ejects a cartridge.
 (4) Pushing forward on the bolt handle seats another cartridge from the magazine into the chamber.
 (5) Turning the handle down after pushing the bolt assembly forward, will lock the breech ready for firing.

b. Bolt Stop (fig. 28). The bolt stop is located at the left rear of the receiver. Pressing inward on the bolt stop will release the stop from the left hand locking lug on the bolt, al lowing bolt to be withdrawn from the receive To install the bolt, press inward on the bolt sto and slide the bolt into receiver well.

c. Magazine.
 (1) The magazine holds five cal..30-06 cartridges. It is loaded through opening in the top front part of the receiver.
 (2) To load a cartridge into the magazine (fig. 29), press the cartridge down against the magazine spring pressure until cartridge snaps into the magazine.

d. Magazine Cover Catch (fig. 30).
 (1) The magazine cover catch is located on the forward portion of the trigger guard.
 (2) Depressing the catch releases the magazine cover, and allows cover to swing open and discharge the cartridges. The catch is spring loaded for returning to its original position.

e. Safety Lock.
 (1) *General.* The safety lock (fig. 31) is located at the rear of the bolt. It is knurled and shaped to fit the thumb.

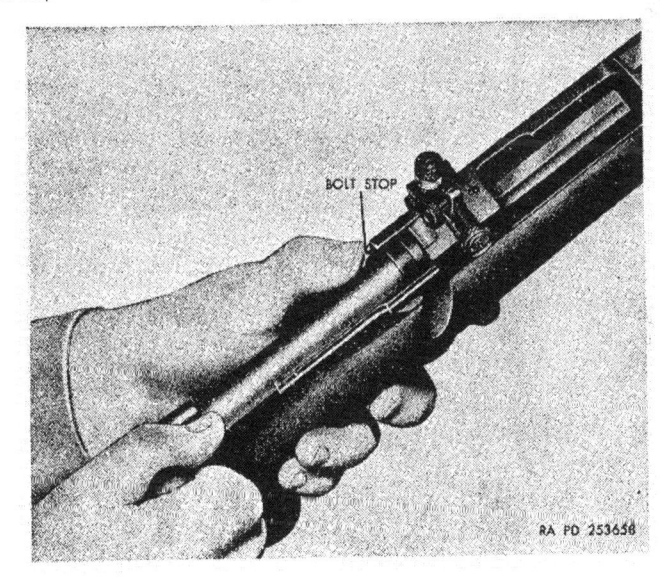

Figure 28. Removing bolt from receiver (Winchester rifle model 70).

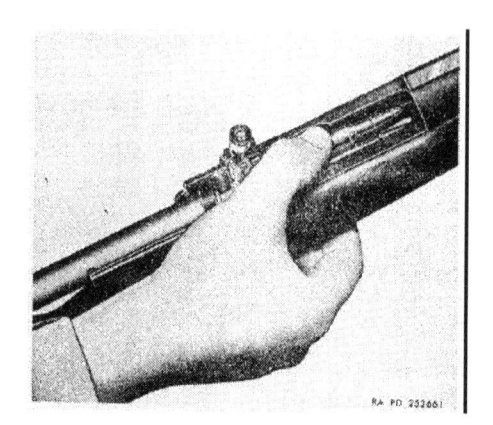

Figure 29. Loading cartridge into magazine (Winchester rifle model 70).

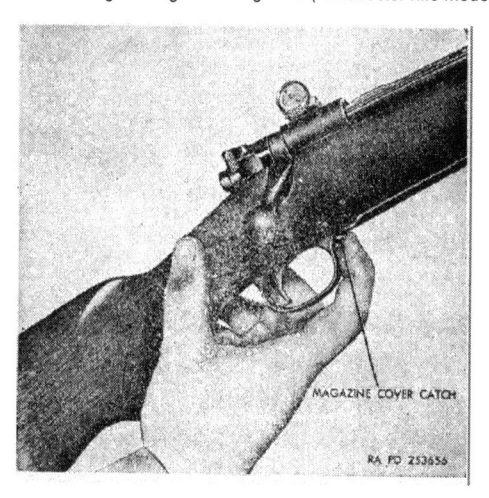

Figure 30. Depressing magazine cover catch (Winchester rifle model 70).

It cannot be operated unless the, firing pin in the bolt assembly has been cocked.
(2) *Full On.* The safety lock is FULL ON when in the rear position in line with the breech bolt. Both the firing pin and bolt are positively locked.
(3) *Intermediate.* The safety lock is in INTERMEDIATE position when at right angles to the bolt. This position locks the firing pin but not the bolt. This allows cartridges to remain in the chamber or to be extracted from the chamber or magazine with safety.
(4) *Fire.* Rifle is ready to be fired when safety lock is full forward.

f. Trigger. The trigger is machined out of a single forging and designed with the sear to give a very short crisp let off with no military take up and with small trigger movement. The trigger pull is adjusted at the factory and will not be adjusted by the shooter.

16. Lyman Rear Sight No. 48WH (fig. 32)

a. General. The Lyman rear sight No. 48WH incorporates micrometer click adjustments for both windage and elevation. The elevation slide group may be quickly removed by turning the locking bolt knob with a screwdriver or coin. The setting on the elevation scale is maintained by the setting of the elevation stop screw. The sight has an elevation scale pointer and windage scale whose positions are adjustable. The setting of elevation and windage are changed by the elevation knob or windage knob.

b. Elevation Knob.
 (1) The elevation knob is located at the top left part of the sight. The knob is marked with a counterclockwise arrow and UP to indicate knob direction to move bullet impact up. It is also marked in eight graduations, one for each click per knob revolution. The index for this scale is on the elevation scale.
 (2) Turning the knob counterclockwise one click, moves point of bullet impact up 1/4 inch for a range of 100 yards.

c. Elevation Scale. The elevation scale located on the sight slide is graduated from 0 to 60. One complete revolution of the elevation knob moves the scale up one division.

d. Elevation Scale Pointer. The elevation scale pointer located at the left of the elevation scale may be adjusted for position by loosening the elevation pointer screw.

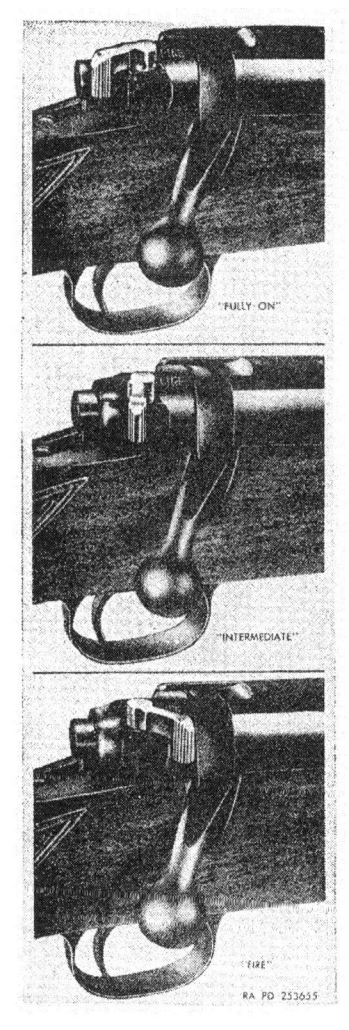

Figure 31. Three positions of safety lock (Winchester rifle model 0).

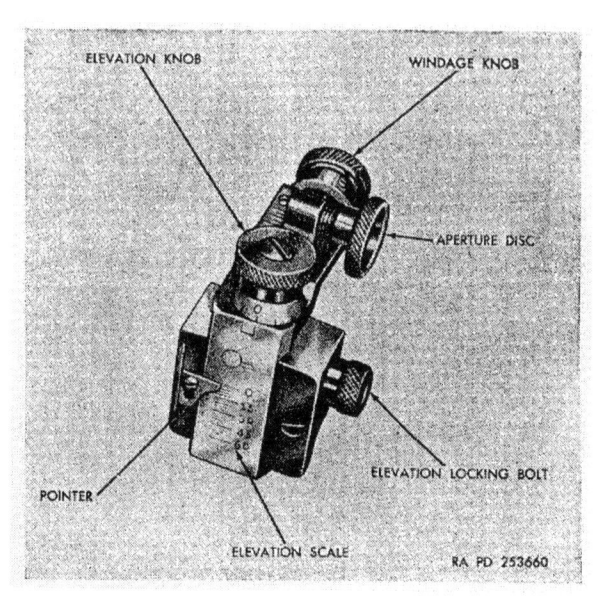

Figure 32. Lyman rear right No. 48WH (Winchester rifle model 70).

e. *Windage Knob.*

(1) The windage knob is located at the right side of the sight slide. The knob is marked with clockwise arrow and L to indicate knob direction to move bullet impact to the left. It is also marked in eight graduations; one for each click per revolution. The index for this scale is on the windage click spring.

(2) Turning the windage knob clockwise, one click, moves point of bullet impact 1/4 inch to the left for a range of 100 yards.

f. *Windage Scale.* The windage scale is graduated from 0 to + 6. The zero position of the scale can be adjusted by loosening the two scale screws. The index mark for the scale is located on the sight aperture.

g. *Rear Sight Aperture Disk.* The rear sight aperture disk is a 5/A:-inch disk with an 0.040-inch hole centrally located. It is screwed into the rear sight slide aperture and can easily be removed for cleaning.

17. **Lyman Target Front Sight No. 77**
(fig. 33)

a. *Description.* The Lyman target front sight No. 77 is a hooded-type sight. It is easily detached from the sight base for cleaning or repair. It then can be returned to exactly the same position by means of an alining slot in the base. The aperture is adjusted by using an interchangeable insert. Nine different styles of insert are supplied to meet the needs of the individual shooter.

b. *Inserts.* To install the insert, unscrew the insert holding nut and install the insert in the slot of the sight hood. Screw in the nut while holding the insert in upright alinement.

c. *Removal and Installation.* To remove the sight from the sight base, loosen the base locking bolt and slide the sight from the rear of the base. Install the sight by sliding the sight on the base and tightening the bolt.

18. **Cal 22 Rifle M12 Receiver Extension Rear Sight Assembly**
(fig. 34)

a. *Description.* A Lyman rear sight No. 525 (or a

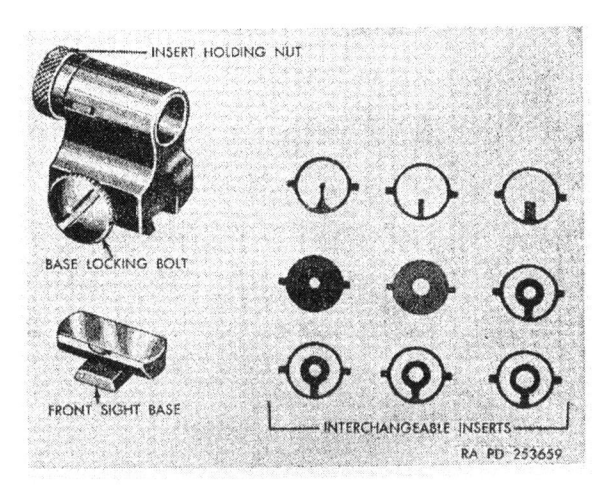

Figure 33. Lyman target front sight (Winchester rifle M70).

Redfield Olympic Receiver sight with number W670 receiver sight base and Master Sighting Disc) is secured by two receiver base mounting screws on the left side of the receiver for M12 rifles. On the front of the rear sight base is stamped 0 which, when in line with the graduated elevation plate on the rear sight slide, gives the elevation to which the sight is set. The rear sight base is machined on the left side to take the rear sight slide, and drilled and tapped to take the rear sight elevation plate screw; the top end of this screw passes through the hole in the slide and secures the slide to the base by means of the elevation knob which slides over the top end of the screw and is retained by an elevation knob setscrew. This knob has a knurled head with a scale beneath it. The scale is marked off in 12 graduations which correspond to the 12 slots or serrations on its underside. These 12 slots engage a raised portion of the click elevation spring. A raised portion on the click engages the slots or serrations of the knob, with the result that, when the elevation knob is turned, a loud click is heard. The rear sight slide is an inverted L-shaped part on the side of which is assembled the graduated elevation plate. The clearance hole in the plate is elongated to provide means of adjustment. The top of the rear sight slide is slotted to receive from the left side the rear sight aperture, windage screw, cap, knob, and click spring. The windage aperture is drilled and tapped to receive the windage screw and moves on its threads and slides on the slot in the slide, when the screw is turned. At the end of the slot, the click spring is installed over the windage cap and is positioned by the heads of the two windage cap screws and retained on the windage screw by the right face of the knob. The raised center portion of the click spring engages the slots in the right face of the knob, so that when the knob is turned, a distinct click is heard. The upper portion of the aperture is drilled and tapped to receive the rear sight disk which is installed at the rear of the aperture. Turning the windage knob moves the aperture and disk to left or right. A graduated windage scale is located at the front top portion of the slide. Its clearance hole is elongated to permit adjustment.

b. Knobs, Scales, and Disk. The elevation and windage knobs, scales, and sight disk on the receiver extension rear sight assembly function similarly to those described in paragraph 16.

AGO 1000A

The construction of the assembly is also similar, although the nomenclature of the parts are slightly different.
   c. *Removal and Installation.*
      (1) Loosen two receiver base mounting screws on left side of receiver and slide sight assembly from base.
      (2) Slide sight assembly on base and secure with two receiver base mounting screws.

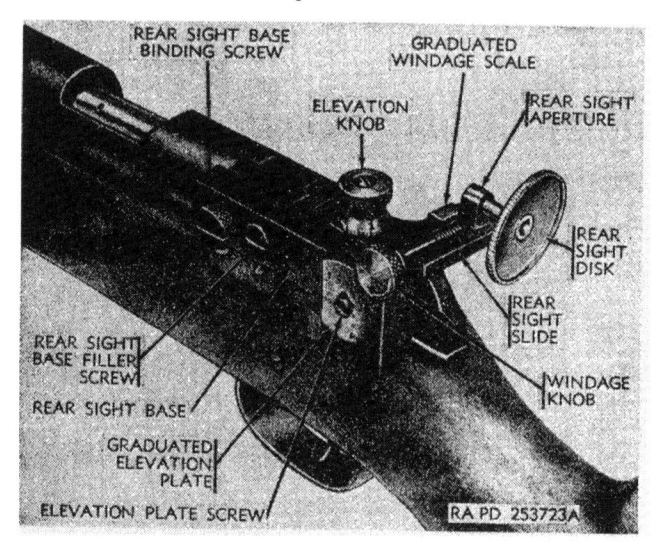

Figure 34. Caliber .22 rifle M12 receiver extension rear sight assembly.

Section III. OPERATION UNDER USUAL CONDITIONS

19. **General**
This section contains instructions for the mechanical steps necessary to operate the weapons under usual conditions.

20. **Cal. .22 High Standard Automatic Pistol (Supermatic)**
   a. *Loading.*
      (1) Place safety lever to SAFE position (par. 10*b*).
      (2) Depress the magazine catch (par. 10*a*).
      (3) Remove the magazine assembly from the pistol.
      (4) Insert 10 cartridges into the magazine assembly (par. 10*c*).
      (5) Insert the magazine assembly into the pistol.
      Note. Catch should hold magazine firmly in the frame.
      (6) Move safety lever to FIRE position (par. 10*b*).
      (7) After previous firing, the slide assembly will be locked in the rearward position. Push the slide lock lever down (par. 10*e*) and allow the slide assembly to strip the first cartridge from the magazine assembly. If the pistol has not been fired, draw back on slide assembly to cock the hammer and proceed as above.
      (8) Set safety lever in SAFE position (par. 10*b*).

AGO 10003A

33

b. *Firing.*
(1) Set safety lever to FIRE position (par. 10*b*).
(2) Aline front sight and rear sight on the 6 o'clock position on the target. The correct sight picture is shown in figure 35. If it is necessary to zero the pistol, refer to paragraph 26.
(3) Squeeze the trigger.
(4) For continuous firing until the magazine is empty, it is only necessary to re-aim as in (2) above and to squeeze the trigger since extraction and ejection of the cartridge case is automatic.

c. *Unloading.*
(1) Depress the magazine catch (par. 10*a*).
(2) Remove the magazine assembly from the pistol (par. 10*c*).
(3) Carefully move slide assembly rearward and lock in this position with slide lock (par. 10*e*). This will extract and eject any cartridge from the chamber.
(4) Examine chamber for any remaining cartridge.
(5) Refer to paragraph 42 for unloading a cartridge after a failure to fire.

21. **Cal. .22 Ruger Mark I Automatic Pistol (Target Model) (6 7/8-In. Barrel)**
a. *Loading.*
(1) Depress the magazine catch (par. 11*b*).
(2) Remove the magazine assembly from the frame.
(3) Insert nine cartridges into the magazine assembly (par . 11*e*).
(4) Insert the magazine assembly into the pistol.
Note. The catch should firmly hold the magazine assembly in the frame.
(5) Move the safety catch to FIRE position (par. 11a).

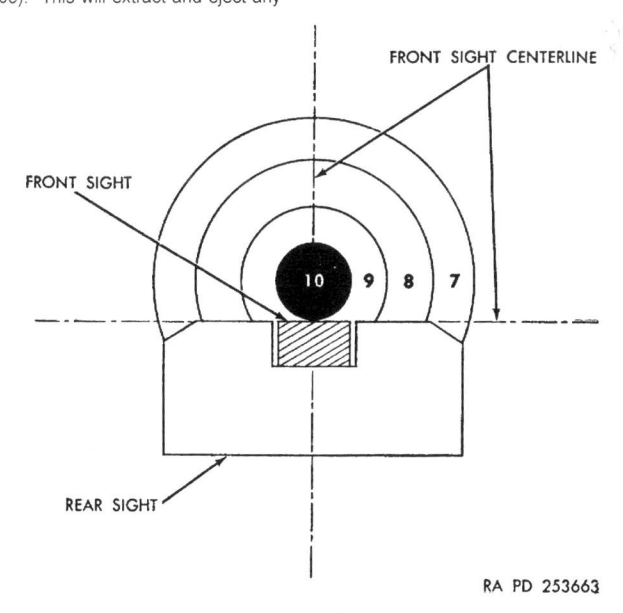

Figure 35. Correct target and sight picture.

AGO 10003A

Figure 36. Inspecting chamber after unloading pistol (Ruger).

    (6) Cock the bolt assembly to feed the first cartridge into the chamber (par. 11c).
- b. *Firing.*
    (1) Set safety catch to FIRE position (par. 11a).
    (2) Aim front sight and rear sight to the 6 o'clock position on the target. The correct sight picture is given in figure 35. If necessary to zero the pistol, refer to paragraph 26.
    (3) Squeeze the trigger.
    (4) For continuous firing with the magazine until it is empty, it is only necessary to aim as in (2) above, and to squeeze the trigger since extraction and ejection of the cartridge case is automatic.
- c. *Unloading.*
    (1) Depress magazine catch (par. 11b).
    (2) Remove magazine assembly from frame; then remove cartridge from magazine (par. 11e).
    (3) Move bolt to rearward position (par. 11c) and set safety catch to SAFE position to lock it there (par. 11a). This should extract and eject any cartridge from the chamber. Examine the chamber for any remaining cartridge (fig. 36).
    (4) Refer to paragraph 42 for unloading after a failure to fire.

22. Cal. .38 Special Smith and Wesson Revolver K-38 (Masterpiece)
- a. *Loading.*
    (1) Depress the thumbpiece (par. 12a) and swing the cylinder and yoke out of the frame (par. 12d).
    (2) If the weapon has been fired previously, press in on the extractor rod (par. 12b) to extract the cartridge cases.
    (3) Insert six rounds into the cylinder (fig. 37).
    (4) Swing the cylinder and yoke into the frame. It should be locked shut by the locking bolt (fig. 37) and the bolt (M, fig. 58).

AGO 10003

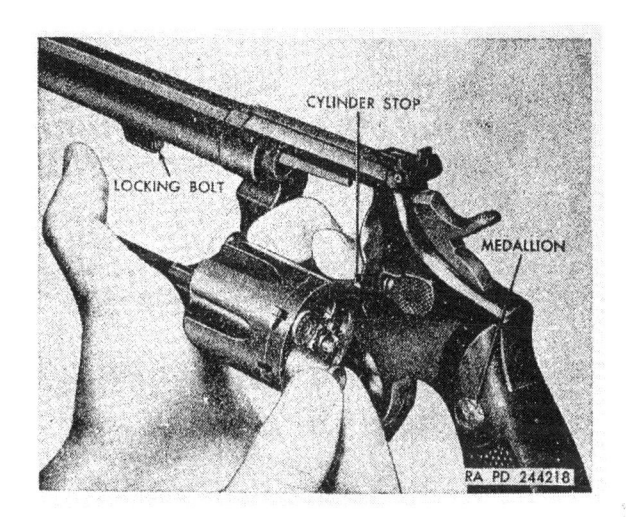

Figure 37. Loading cartridge into cylinder (Smith and Wesson).

b. *Firing.*
(1) Single action.
  (a) If all chambers of the cylinder are not completely loaded, alinement of the proper chamber may be necessary. The first loaded chamber should be on the right of the chamber alined with the barrel. Hold hammer as described in paragraph 12c while alining the chamber.
  (b) Cock the hammer (par. 12c).
  (c) Aim the front and rear sight to the 6 o'clock position on the target. The correct sight picture is shown in figure 35. If zeroing of the revolver is necessary, refer to paragraph 26.
  (d) Squeeze the trigger.
  (e) For continuous firing, repeat (b) through (d) above until six cartridges in cylinder have been fired.
(2) *Double action.*
  (a) If chamber is improperly alined, proceed as described in (1) (a) above.
  (b) Cock hammer by pulling back on the trigger (par. 12f (1)).
  (c) Aim front and rear sights ((1) (c) above).
  (d) Squeeze trigger further until hammer falls.
  (e) For continuous firing repeat (b) through (d) above until cylinder is empty.

c. *Unloading.*
(1) If hammer has been cocked, lower it as described in paragraph 12c(4).
(2) Depress the thumbpiece (par. 12a) and swing the cylinder and yoke out of the frame (par. 12d).
(3) Press in on extractor rod and carefully remove cartridges.
(4) Refer to paragraph 42 for unloading after a failure to fire.

23. Cal. .22 Rifle M12 (Winchester Rifle Model 52, Heavy Barrel)

a. *Loading.*
(1) Lift the breech bolt handle and pull all the way to the rear (par. 13a).
(2) Insert five cartridges in the magazine (par. 13b). A sixth cartridge may be loaded by hand into the chamber while holding down

AGO 10003A

36

on the magazine before pushing the bolt forward.

(3) Push bolt handle forward and lock the bolt (par. 13a).

Warning: **Place the safety lever on SAFE immediately after the rifle is fully loaded. Do not touch the trigger while loading or shift the position of the safety, in order to prevent premature firing.**

b. *Firing.*
 (1) Place safety lever in FIRE position.
 (2) Aim for the 6 o'clock position on the target, using disk aperture of receiver sight and the insert of front sight. If zeroing is necessary, refer to paragraph 26.
 (3) Squeeze the trigger.
 (4) To continue firing, eject the cartridge case and repeat (2) and (3) above until magazine has been emptied.

c. *Unloading.*
 (1) Place safety lever on FIRE position.
 (2) Open bolt and extract cartridge from chamber.
 (3) Release base from magazine and remove cartridges.

24. **Cal. .22 Rifle M12 (Remington Rifle Model 40X-S1)**
 a. *Loading.*
  (1) Put the safety on FIRE and lift the bolt handle (par. 14a) and pull all the way to the rear.
  (2) Insert one cartridge by hand in the chamber of the rifle. This is a one shot weapon.
  (3) Push the bolt forward and turn the bolt handle down to locked position.
  (4) Put the safety on SAFE (par. 14d).
 b. *Firing.*
  (1) Place safety in FIRE position.
  (2) Aim for the 6 o'clock position on the target, using disk aperture of receiver sight and the insert of front sight. If zeroing is necessary, refer to paragraph 26.
  (3) Squeeze the trigger.
  (4) To continue firing, reload (*a* above) and fire (*b*(1), (2), and (3) above).

25. **Cal. .30-06 Winchester Rifle Model 70 (Special Match Grade)**
 a. *Loading.*
  (1) Pull bolt fully rearward (par. 15a).
  (2) Insert five cartridges into the magazine (par. 15c). A sixth cartridge may be loaded into chamber (fig. 38) if necessary, while holding down on the magazine before starting bolt forward.
  (3) Push bolt forward and lock the bolt (par. 15a).
  (4) Place safety lock to FULLY ON position (par. 15e).

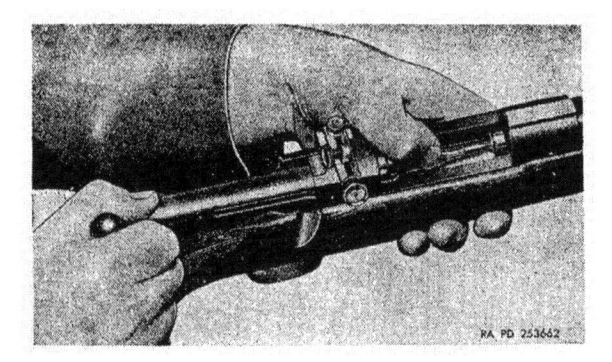

Figure 38. Loading cartridge into chamber (Winchester rifle M70).

b. *Firing.*
(1) Move safety lock to FIRE position (par. 15e).
(2) Aim for the 6 o'clock position on the target, using disk aperture of rear sight and insert of front sight. If zeroing is necessary, refer to paragraph 26.
(3) Squeeze the trigger.
(4) To continue firing, eject the cartridge (par. 15a(3)), load another cartridge into chamber from magazine (par. 15a(4)), and repeat (2) and (3) above until magazine has been emptied.

c. *Unloading.*
(1) Place safety lock to FULLY ON position (par. 15e).
(2) Depress magazine cover catch and open magazine cover to remove cartridges (fig. 39) remaining in magazine.
(3) Place safety lock on INTERMEDIATE position (par. 15e).
(4) Remove any cartridge remaining in chamber by withdrawing bolt (par. 15a(3)).
(5) Refer to paragraph 42 for unloading after a failure to fire.

26. Target Zeroing

a. *Pistols and Revolvers.* Each weapon has individual characteristics which may require correction, by the shooter, of the rear sight adjustment in order to bring the point of bullet impact inside the center of the target. These weapons have been zeroed by the manufacturer at the factory at targets and ranges which do not correspond to the National Match competition targets and ranges. For greatest competitive accuracy, the weapons should be zeroed at these distances. A normal day with little or no wind blowing should be selected. Fire a group of three rounds and note the point of impact on the center of the group on the target. Shift the point of impact vertically and horizontally by adjusting the rear sight windage adjustments (pars. 10g, 11d(3), 12h, or 16e) and elevation adjustments (pars. 10g(2), 11d(2), 12g, or 16b. The shift of bullet impact for each click will depend also on the target range; if

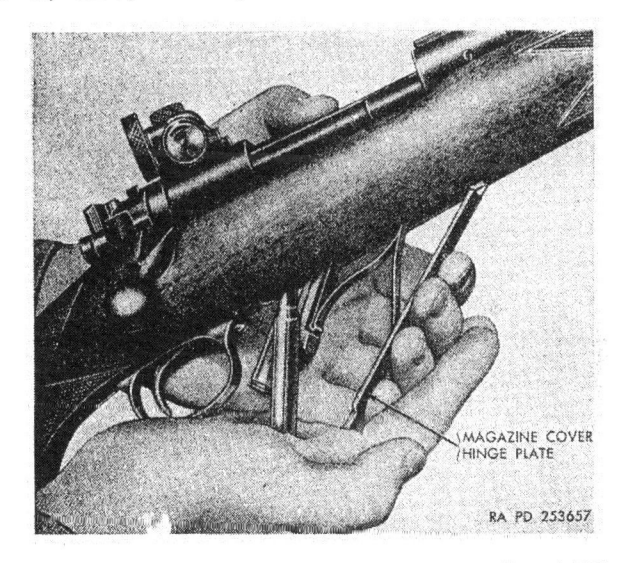

Figure 39. Unloading cartridge from magazine (Winchester rifle model 70).

AGO 10003A

for example, the range is doubled or half that given in the above paragraphs, the shift will be doubled or halved. After the sights have been adjusted, shoot another group of three rounds and note the point of impact of the center of the group. Readjust the sights again if necessary. On the Winchester rifle Model 70, set the elevation scale pointer (par. 16d) at zero and windage scale (par. 16f) at index mark after the rifle has been targeted.

    b. Rear Sight Setting for M12 Rifles. The rear sights of the M12 rifles covered in this manual are provided with elevating and windage screws for shifting the aperture in the rear sight disk for elevation or windage settings. These screws are furnished with knobs which, when turned, are retained in position by click springs (or like parts) or retaining balls seating in notches in the face of the knobs. The seating of the click spring or balls can be plainly heard or felt as the knobs are turned. The relation between the pitch of the screw threads and the notches in the knobs is such that each notch corresponds to a shift in the aperture in the rear sight disk vertically or laterally measured in minutes of angle. Each minute of angle corresponds to a shift of the point of impact of the bullet on the target in inches, varying with the range or distance of the target. These fractional shifts of the knobs are called "clicks." In the rifles covered herein, each click corresponds either to 1/4 or 1/2 minute change in angle of sight; such changes correspond to a 1/4 or 1/2 inch shift of the point of impact of the bullet on the target at 100 yards. This shift varies with the distance; as the range is doubled or halved, the amount of shift of the point of impact is doubled or halved. Thus, in a sight having 1/4-click graduations, the point of impact will be shifted 1/16 inch at 25 yards, 1/8 inch at 50 yards, 1/4 inch at -100 yards, and 1/2 inch at 200 yards, etc. Likewise, in a sight having 1/2-click graduations, the point of impact will be shifted 1/8 inch at 25 yards, 1/4, inch at 50 yards, and 1/2 inch at 100 yards, etc., in the same ratio. Turning the elevating screw knob (or like part) shifts the point of impact vertically and turning the windage screw knob (or like part) shifts the point of impact laterally. The sights are usually adjusted at the factory, but to make sure they are correct, they should be checked on the range.

Section IV. OPERATION UNDER UNUSUAL CONDITIONS

27. General

    The mechanical steps of operation under unusual conditions are the same for operation under usual conditions as explained in paragraphs 19 through 26. The only difference in procedure is in the servicing of the weapons with regard to cleaning and' lubrication to insure proper functioning in locations where extremes of atmosphere, temperature, and humidity occur. Special care will be observed with regard to the cleaning and lubrication of the weapon. Such care is necessary to insure proper operation and functioning of the weapons, and to guard against excessive wear of the moving parts and deterioration of the materiel.

28. Extreme Cold Weather Conditions

    Match competition would not be scheduled under such conditions.

29. Operation in Extreme Hot Weather Conditions

    a. In hot climates, the thin film of oil necessary for weapons under normal conditions will be quickly dissipated. Inspect weapons frequently, renew oil film as often as is necessary to prevent rusting, and assure the gun being ready for firing. Clean weapons frequently and remove grit or dust which sticks to oiled surfaces.

    b. Keep weapons covered as much as possible.

    c. Perspiration from the hands is a contributing factor to rusting, because perspiration contains acid. When handled, weapons should be wiped dry frequently, and the oil film maintained.

    d. When weapons are not to be used for a long period of time (20 days or more) they should be cleaned

AGO 10003A

with rifle bore cleaner, and then lubricated with special preservative lubricating oil. Remove all excess oil from core and chamber before firing.

  e. Where the humidity is high, take special care to inspect unexposed surfaces such as the bore, chamber, and like places, where rusting might occur and not be quickly noted. Watch screws and pins to prevent rust attacking and freezing them in place.

30. Excessive Sandy or Dusty Conditions

  a. In localities where dust and sandstorms are prevalent, weapons should be carefully covered at all times. Dust and sand will enter the mechanisms and bore. It will stick on lubricated surfaces, forming a gummy paste that may clog the weapons and cause malfunction. This paste will also act as an abrasive and will cause undue wear on the moving parts of the weapons.

  b. Under such conditions the weapons should be field stripped (pars. 45 through 50), cleaned (par. 38), and lubricated (par. 36) as often as practical.

AGO 10008A

Lubrication should be confined to moving parts and contacting surfaces, and should be as light as possible for proper functioning of the weapon. Remove all excess oil from bore and chamber before firing.

31. Excessive Moist or Salty Atmosphere

  a. Salt air is conducive to quick rusting as the salt has a tendency to emulsify the oil and destroy its rust-preventive qualities. The weapons should be inspected frequently, kept lightly lubricated and treated in a manner similar to that prescribed for weapons in hot climates (par. 29).

  b. If weapons are not to be used for a prolonged period (20 days or more), they should be cleaned (par. 38) and lubricated with special preservative lubricating oil. Remove all excess oil from bore and chamber before firing.

CHAPTER 3
PREVENTIVE MAINTENANCE INSTRUCTIONS

Section I. PARTS, SPECIAL TOOLS, AND EQUIPMENT FOR OPERATION AND PREVENTIVE MAINTENANCE

32. General

Tools and equipment are issued to the user for operating and maintaining the materiel. Tools and equipment should not be used for purposes other than prescribed and, when not in use, should be properly stored in the case or box provided for them.

33. Parts

Spare parts for National Match rifles, revolvers, and pistols are listed in SB 9-112, SB 9-125, and SB 9-135 for procurement needed from unit funds for installation by the unit gunsmith. They are not stored by Ordnance Supply. Commercial match, rifles, pistols, and revolvers and equipment requiring repair beyond the scope of the gunsmith will be returned direct to the manufacturer for repair and returned to the user when repaired, utilizing appropriated funds available to the unit. Tools and equipment supplied for the weapons are listed in ORD 7 SNL B49 for Cal. .22 high standard automatic pistol (supermatic) and Cal. .22 Ruger automatic pistol (target model); ORD 7 SNL B29 for Cal. .38 special, K38 master, piece, Smith and Wesson revolver; ORD 7 SNL B25 for Cal. .22 Winchester rifle Model 52 heavy barrel and ORD 7 SNL B50 for Cal. .30-06 Winchester rifle Model 70, or other Department of the Army supply manuals, which are the authority for requisitioning replacements.

34. Common Tools and Equipment

Common tools and equipment having general application to this materiel are authorized for issue by tables of allowances and tables of organization and equipment.

35. Special Tools and Equipment

Special tools and equipment designed for operation, and maintenance, repair, and general use with the materiel are listed in table I for information only. This list is not to be used for requisitioning replacements.

Table I. Special Tools and Equipment For Operation and Preventive Maintenance

Item	Identifying No.	References Figure	References Paragraph	Use
a. Rifle, Cal. .30-06 Winchester, Model 70 (Special Match Grade).				
BRUSH, WIRE, TUBE, cleaning, cal. .30	5564174	42	38	To clean rifle bore.
CASE, cleaning rod, cal. .30	7162792	42	38	To hold cleaning rod.
CASE, plastic	5621060	42	38	To hold oiler.
ROD, cleaning, cal. .30, M10	7162920	42	38	To clean bore of rifle.
SLING STRAP: 3258 for 1 1/4-in. bows	WRA-13170	H, 51	----------	To steady the rifle.
b. Pistol, Automatic, Cal. .22, High Standard (Supermatic) and Pistol, Automatic, Cal. .22, Ruger Mark I (Target Model) (6 7/8-in. bbl).				
ROD, cleaning, pistol. cal. .22	17162231	40	38	To clean bore of pistol.

AGO 10003A

Table 1. Special Tools and Equipment For Operation and Preventive Maintenance-Continued

Item	Identifying No.	References Figure	References Paragraph	Use
c. Revolver, Smith and Wesson, Cal. .38, Special, K-38 (Masterpiece).				
BRUSH, copper	SW-5115-1	41	38	To clean bore and cylinder.
HANDLE, cleaning rod	SW-5115-2	41	38	To hold copper brush or cleaning swab.
SCREWDRIVER	SW-5193	41	47	To adjust rear sight and field strip weapon.
SWAB, cleaning		41	38	To clean bore and cylinder.
d. Rifle, Cal. .22, M12.				
BRUSH: cleaning, cal. .22, M3	5564179	43	38	Clean bore and cylinder.
CASE: assy (oiler and thong)	5621060	43	36	To hold oiler.
GREASE: rifle, lubr (RG) 5-cc cntr 14 G-1435-910.			40	Lubricate rifle.
ROD: cleaning, Cal. .22, M1	5503837	43	38	To push brush through bore.
SLING: gun, M1 (webbing)	6544058	43	40	To steady rifle.
SCREWDRIVER, RIFLE	5564038	43		Adjust or remove bolts and screws.

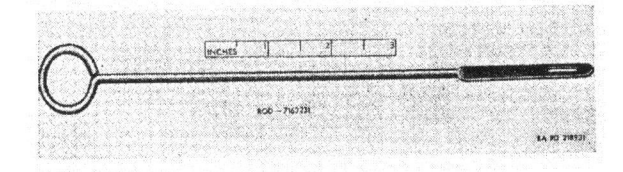

Figure 40. Special tools and equipment (High Standard and Ruger).

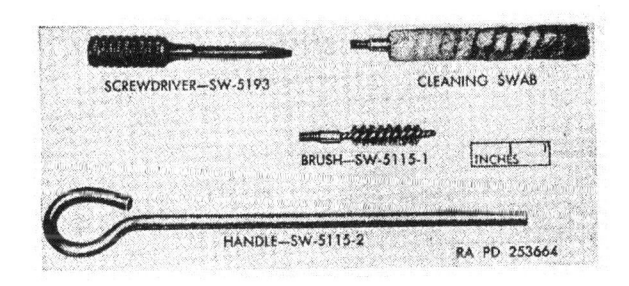

Figure 41. Special tools and equipment (Smith and Wesson).

AGO 10003A

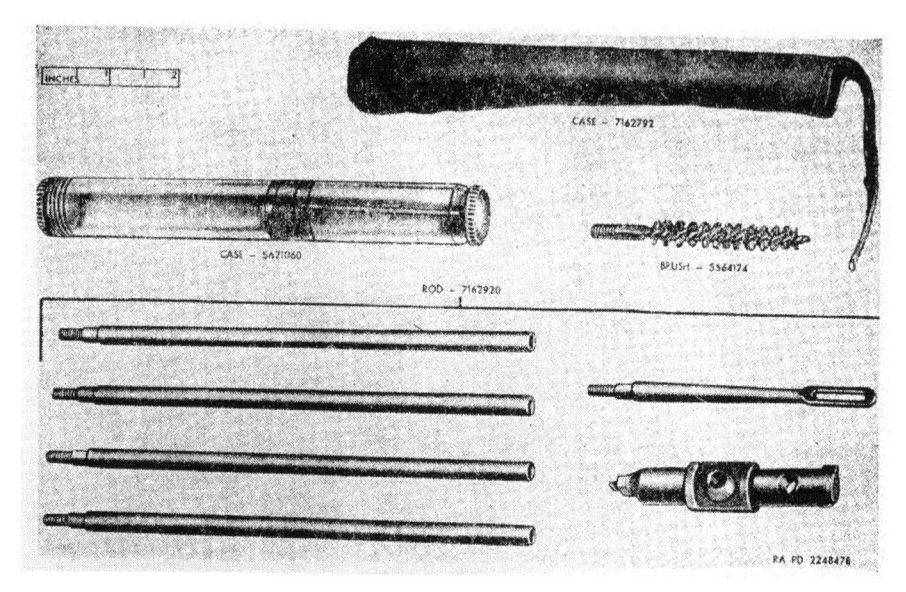

Figure 42. Special tools and equipment (Winchester rifle model 70).

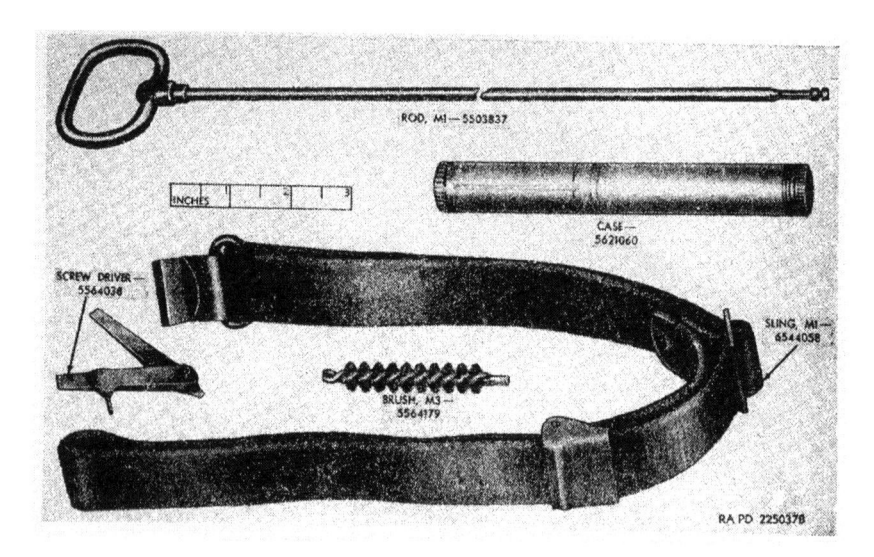

Figure 43. Special tools and equipment (Cal. .22 rifles).

AGO 10003A

Section II. LUBRICATION AND PREVENTIVE MAINTENANCE SERVICES

36. Lubrication

a. General. The lubrication charts prescribe cleaning and lubrication procedures as to points to be lubricated, intervals, and lubricants to be used under various conditions.

b. Pistol, Automatic, Cal. .22, High Standard (Supermatic).

Slide assembly -------- Weekly and after firing, clean with rifle-bore cleaner (CR). Dry and oil with PL special.

Bore and chamber ---- Immediately after firing and on two consecutive days thereafter, thoroughly clean with CR, making sure that all surfaces, including the rifling, are well coated. Do not wipe dry. On the third day after firing, clean with CR, wipe dry and lightly coat with PL. Weekly, there-after, when weapon is not being fired, clean with CR, wipe dry and reoil with PL. Wipe clean before firing.

Frame group ---------- Clean with dry-cleaning and solvent or mineral-spirits paint thinner, dry thoroughly, and apply a light coat of PL special.

magazine assembly.

CR—Cleaner, rifle-bore
PL—Oil, lubricating, preservative

c. Pistol, Automatic, Cal. .22, Ruger Mark I (Target Model) (6 7/8-In. Barrel).

Bolt assembly -------- Weekly and after firing, clean with rifle-bore cleaner (CR). Dry and oil with PL special.

Bore, chamber, ------- Immediately after firing and on two consecutive days thereafter, thoroughly clean with CR, making sure that all surfaces, including the rifling, are well coated. Do not wipe dry. On the third day after firing, clean with CR, wipe dry and lightly coat with PL. Weekly, thereafter, when weapon is not being fired, clean with CR, wipe dry and reoil with PL. Wipe clean before firing.

and receiver.

Frame group ---------- Clean with dry-cleaning solvent or mineral-spirits paint thinner, dry thoroughly, and apply a light coat of PL special.

and magazine assembly.

CR—Cleaner, rifle-bore
PL—Oil, lubricating, preservative

d. Revolver, Smith and Wesson, Cal. .38, Special, K-39 (Masterpiece).

Firing mechanism ---- Weekly and after firing, clean with rifle-bore cleaner (CR). Dry and oil with PL special.

Bore and cylinder ----- Immediately after firing and on two consecutive days thereafter, thoroughly clean with CR, making sure that all surfaces, including the rifling, are well coated. Do not wipe dry. On the third day after firing, clean with CR, wipe dry and lightly coat with PL. Weekly, there-after, when weapon is not being fired, clean with CR, wipe dry and reoil with PL. Wipe clean before firing.

CR—Cleaner, rifle-bore
PL—Oil, lubricating, preservative

e. Rifle, Cal. .22, M12 and Cal. .30-06.

Bolt assembly and ---- Weekly and after firing, clean with rifle-bore cleaner (CR). Dry and oil with PL special.

receiver.

AGO 10003A

Bore and chamber---- Immediately after firing and on two consecutive days thereafter, thoroughly clean with CR, making sure that all surfaces, including the rifling, are well coated. Do not wipe dry. On the third day after firing, clean with CR, wipe dry and lightly coat with PL. Weekly, there-after, when weapon is not being fired, clean with CR, wipe dry and reoil with PL. Wipe clean before firing.

Firing group ---------- Clean with dry-cleaning solvent or mineral-spirits paint thinner, dry thoroughly, and apply a light coat of PL special.

Sling (M1907)---------- Weekly clean and soften leather leather. with NF. Wipe thoroughly dry.

CR—Cleaner, rifle-bore
PL—Oil, lubricating, preservative
NF—Oil, Neat's-foot

  f. Special Lubrication Instructions.
  (1) Lubrication should be accomplished carefully and sparingly. All excess oil should be wiped from the weapons. This is especially important with regard to the barrel, chamber, and recoiling parts.
  Caution: **Oil or grease in the chamber or barrel will raise the breech pressure and may result in damage to materiel and injury to personnel.**
  (2) Special preservative lubricating oil will be used at all temperatures for metallic parts of the weapon.
  (3) Neat's-foot oil will be used for cleaning and softening the leather sling of the Winchester rifle. Use it sparingly, rub it in well, and wipe it off carefully.
  (4) Remove excess oil from the bore and chamber of the barrel before firing. Smoking of the weapon may indicate excessive lubrication.

37. **General**

AGO 10003A

Preventive-maintenance services prescribed by Army regulations are a function of using organization level of maintenance. This section contains preventive-maintenance services allocated to operating personnel and to organizational maintenance personnel.

38. **Cleaning**
  a. General.
  (1) Rifle-bore cleaner is used for cleaning the weapon, after it has been fired, or for periodic cleaning as outlined in preventive-maintenance services (par. 39).
  (2) Rifle-bore cleaner contains volatile solvents that evaporate at temperatures above 150° F., thus reducing the cleaning action. Therefore, after firing, the weapon should not be cleaned until it has cooled to the point where the barrel can be touched with the bare hand.
  (3) Maximum cleaning efficiency and protection against rusting will be obtained, when rifle-bore cleaner is used undiluted.
  b. Daily. Inspect bore and chamber for rust and remove accumulated dirt or other foreign matter.
  c. Before Firing.
  (1) Thoroughly clean the bore and chamber of all dirt or foreign matter. Run a clean patch through the bore to remove surplus oil.
  (2) Wipe outer surfaces of the weapon, using a clean wiping cloth wet with proper oil and wrung out.
  d. After Firing. The cleaning procedures prescribed in (1) through (4) below are to be followed at the end of the day's firing. If no further firing is anticipated, it is to be repeated on two consecutive days thereafter.
  (1) *Bore and chamber of all rifles.* Place flannel cotton patches in slot of rod and saturate with rifle-bore cleaner, and move through the barrel several times. If rust or foreign matter is not removed by the cleaner, attach the brush 5564174 (fig. 42) and move it several times through the

45

barrel. Make certain the brush goes all the way through, before reversing the direction. A light coating of rifle-bore cleaner should be allowed to remain in the bore and chamber between cleaning.

(2) *Bore and chamber of Smith and Wesson revolver.* Attach cleaning swab (fig. 44) to the handle SW-5115-2 (fig. 44) and dip in rifle-bore cleaner. Move the swab back and forth several times in the bore of the barrel and in chamber of the cylinder (fig. 44). If rust or foreign matter is not removed, attach brush SW-5115-1 (fig. 45) to the handle and run the brush several times through the barrel (fig. 45) and cylinder. A light coating of rifle-bore cleaner should be allowed to remain in the bore and chamber between cleaning.

(3) *Bore and chamber of High-Standard and Ruger Mark I automatic pistols.* Place flannel cotton patch in the slot of the rod 7162231 (fig. 40) and saturate it with rifle-bore cleaner. Move the rod back and forth several times in the barrel. A light coating of riflebore cleaner should be allowed to remain in the bore and chamber between cleaning.

(4) *Parts other than barrel.*
 (a) With rifle-bore cleaner, thoroughly clean all surfaces that have been exposed to powder gases.

 (b) During firing, hard carbon gradually accumulates on parts of the weapon. This deposit must be carefully removed with a scraper or crocus cloth and the parts lubricated immediately.

 (c) Dirt and foreign matter must be removed from all other parts. Thoroughly dry all components and immediately apply a light coating of special preservative lubricating oil. Handle cleaned parts with gloved hands as perspiration from the hands, which contains acid, accelerates corrosion.

e. Service Periods Up to 1 Week. If weapons have not been fired, renew the oil film in the bore and chamber weekly using a flannel cotton cloth saturated in special preservative lubricating oil.

39. General Procedures

The general preventive maintenances described in *a* through *f* below will be observed in addition to schedules in paragraph 40.

a. The importance of a thorough knowledge of how to clean and lubricate materiel cannot be overemphasized. The kind of attention given to

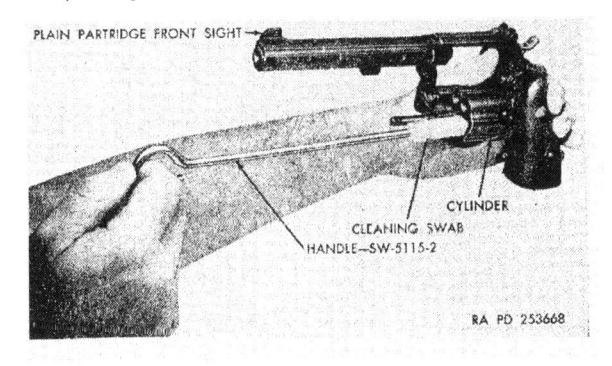

Figure 44. Cleaning cylinder (Smith and Wesson).

AGO 10003A

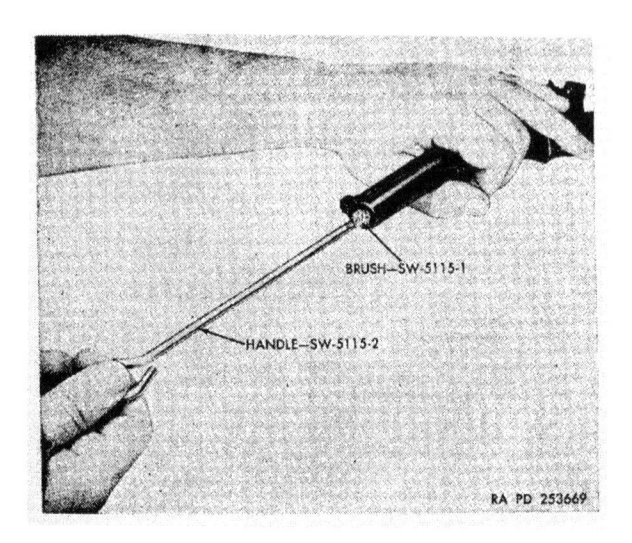

Figure 45. Cleaning barrel (Smith and Wesson).

this gun largely determines whether the gun will shoot accurately and function properly when needed.

 b. Rust, dirt, grit, gummed oil, and water cause rapid deterioration of all parts of the materiel. Particular care should be taken to keep all bearing surfaces and exposed parts clean and properly lubricated. Wiping cloths, rifle bore cleaner, and lubricants are furnished for this purpose. Remove all traces of rust from surfaces with crocus cloth, which is the coarsest abrasive to be used by using personnel for this purpose. Maintenance personnel are authorized the use of stones for honing purposes.

 c. Spare parts, tools, and equipment will be inspected for completeness and serviceability.
Missing or damaged items will be replaced or turned in for repair. Use only tools that are provided and see that they fit properly. Tools that do not fit will fail and cause damage to parts.

 d. No alteration or modification will be made except as authorized by official publications.

 e. Each time the weapon is field stripped, carefully inspect all parts for cracks, wear, rust, and like defects which might cause a malfunction of the weapon.

 f. Each time a weapon is assembled after field stripping, it should be given an operational check by cocking the weapon and dry firing except cal..22 rifles. When possible, a dummy round should be used to check feeding, extraction, chambering, and ejection.

40. Preventive-Maintenance Schedule

 a. To insure continued satisfactory performance, it is necessary that the weapon be inspected periodically, in order that defects may be discovered and corrected before they result in serious damage or failure. Any defects or unsatisfactory operating characteristics beyond the scope of correction by the operator must be reported to the designated authority.

 b. The services set forth in table II are to be performed by the shooter.

Table II. Preventive-Maintenance Schedule

Points of inspection	Detailed instructions
Before Firing	
a. CaL.22 High-Standard Automatic Pistol (Supermatic)	
(1) Clean bore and chamber	Par. 38c
(2) Wipe excess oil from slide assembly and frame group	Par. 38c
(3) Clean outer surfaces of weapon	Par. 38
(4) Check pistol for proper lubrication	Par. 36b
(5) Check operation of safety lever, slide lock lever, and slide assembly	Par. 10
(6) Check magazine assembly for proper installation	Par. 10
(7) Barrel should be held securely by barrel lock and barrel plunger cam	Par. 45b
b. Cal 22 Ruger Mark I Automatic Pistol (Target Model) (67/s-In. Barrel)	
(1) Clean bore and chamber	Par. 38c
(2) Wipe excess oil from bolt assembly, receiver frame group, and mainspring housing	Par. 38c
(3) Clean outer surfaces of pistol	Par. 38c
(4) Check pistol for proper lubrication	Par. 36e
(-;) Check operation of safety catch and bolt assembly	Par. 11
(6) Check magazine for proper installation	Par. 11
(7) Check that barrel and receiver is secured to frame and held by the main-spring housing assembly.	Par. 46b
c. Cal 3S Special, Smith and Wesson Revolver K-38 (Masterpiece)	
(1) Clean bore and cylinder	Par. 38c
(2) Clean outer surfaces of revolver	Par. 38c
(3) Check revolver for proper lubrication	Par. 36d
(4) Check operation of locking bolt, extractor rod, cylinder and yoke, thumb piece, and hammer.	Par. 12
(5) Check cylinder for alignment and tightness	Par. 12
d. Cal 22 Rifles M12 and Cal 30-06 Winchester Rifle, Model 70 (Special Match Grade)	
(1) Clean bore and chamber	Par. 38c
(2) Clean outer surfaces of rifle	Par. 38c
(3) Check rifle for proper lubrication	Par. 36d
(4) Check operation of bolt assembly, magazine, safety lock, and bolt stop	Par. 15
(5) Check front sight for proper aperture	Par. 17
(6) Check rear sight for solid mounting on sight base	Par. 16
(7) Check sling for proper installation	Par. 50b
After Firing	
a. Cal 22 High Standard Automatic Pistol (Supermatic)	
(1) Remove cartridge from magazine assembly and chamber	Par. 20c
(2) Clean and lubricate bore and chamber	Par. 38d(4)
(3) Remove carbon deposits from slide assembly and receiver	Par. 38d(4)
(4) Report any malfunctions to unit gunsmith	Par. 43
(5) Preserve weapon, if further firing is not anticipated	Par. 38
b. Cal 22 Ruger Mark I Automatic Pistol (Target Model) (67/s-In. Barrel)	
(1) Remove cartridge from magazine assembly and chamber	Par. 21c
(2) Remove residue from bolt assembly	Par. 38d(4)
(3) Clean and lubricate bore and chamber	Par. 38d(3)
(4) Report any malfunctions to unit gunsmith	Par. 43
(5) Preserve weapon if further firing is not anticipated	Par. 38e
C. Cal 38 Special, Smith and Wesson Revolver K-38 (Masterpiece)	
(1) Remove cartridge from cylinder	Par. 22c
(2) Remove carbon deposits from cylinder and frame	Par. 38
(3) Clean and lubricate barrel and cylinder	Par. 38d(2)
(4) Report any malfunction to unit gunsmith	Par. 43
(5) Preserve weapon, if further firing is not anticipated	Par. 38e

AGO 10003A

Table II. Preventive-Maintenance Services-Continued

Points of inspection	Detailed instructions
After Firing-Continued	
d. CaL2 M12 and Cal 30-06 Rifles	
(1) Remove cartridge from magazine and from chamber	Par. 25
(2) Remove-residue from bolt assembly and receiver	Par. 38d(3)
(3) Clean and lubricate bore and chamber	Par. 38d(1)
(4) Report any malfunction to unit gunsmith	Par. 43
(5) Preserve weapon if further firing is not anticipated	Par. 38e

Section III. TROUBLESHOOTING

41. General

A malfunction is an improper or faulty action of some component part of the weapon that may result in failure to fire, stoppage, or damage to the weapon.

42. Failure to Fire

a. *Misfires, Hangfires, and Cook-Offs.*

(1) *Misfire.* A misfire is a complete failure to fire, which may be due to a faulty firing mechanism or ammunition. A misfire in itself is not dangerous, but since it cannot be immediately distinguished from a delay in the functioning of the firing mechanism or from a hangfire ((2) below), it should be considered as a possible delayed firing until such possibility has been eliminated. Such delay in the functioning of the firing mechanism, for example, could result from the presence of foreign matter such as grit, sand, frost, ice, or improper or excessive oil or grease, which might create initially a partial mechanical restraint which, after some indeterminate delay, is overcome as a result of the continued force applied by the spring, and the firing pin then driven into the primer in the normal manner. In this connection, no cartridge should be left in a hot weapon any longer than the circumstances require, because of the possibility of a cook-off ((3) below).

(2) *Hangfire.* A hangfire is a delay in the functioning of ammunition at the time of firing. The amount of the delay is unpredictable, but in most cases will fall within the range of a split second to several minutes. Thus, a hangfire cannot be distinguished immediately from a misfire and therein lies the principal danger-that of assuming that a failure of the weapon to fire immediately upon actuation of the firing mechanism is a misfire, whereas in fact it may prove to be a hangfire. It is for this reason that the time intervals prescribed in b below should be observed before opening the bolt after a failure to fire. These time intervals, based on experience and considerations of safety, have been established to minimize the danger associated with a hangfire and to prevent the occurrence of a cook-off.

Caution: **During the prescribed time intervals, the weapon will be kept trained on the target and all personnel will stand clear of the muzzle.**

(3) *Cook-off.* A cook-off is a functioning of any or all of the explosive components of a cartridge chambered in a very hot weapon due to heat from the weapon.

Note. There is little chance of cook-off in these weapons, due to manner in which they are fired.

b. *Procedures for Removing a Cartridge in case of Failure to Fire.*

(1) *General.* After a failure to fire, due to the possibility of a hangfire or cookoff (a (2) and (3) above), the following general precautions, as applicable, will be observed until the cartridge has been

removed from the weapon and the cause of failure determine.

(a) Keep the weapon trained on the target and all personnel clear of the muzzle.

(b) Wait 10 seconds; then extract and eject the cartridge.

(c) The cartridge, after removal from the weapon, will be kept separate from other cartridges until it has been determined whether the cartridge or the firing mechanism was at fault. If the cartridge is determined to be at fault it will continue to be kept separate from other cartridges until disposed of. On the other hand, if examination reveals that the firing mechanism was at fault, the cartridge may be reloaded and fired after correction of the faulty firing mechanism.

(d) The definite time intervals for waiting after failure of weapons to fire prescribed for particular classes of weapons ((2) through (4) below) have been established on the basis of experience and depending on the characteristics of the particular weapon and type of ammunition.

(2) *Bolt-operated rifle.* After a failure to fire, in the case of the rifle which can be recocked without opening the bolt, recock (par. 15a(2)) and make one additional attempt to fire. If the weapon still fails to fire, wait 10 seconds, before opening the bolt (par.15a(3)) to remove the cartridge.

(3) *Revolver.* The weapon cannot be recocked to fire the same cartridge. Wait 10 seconds from the failure to fire before opening the cylinder (par. 12d) and actuating the extractor rod (par.12b) to remove the cartridges.

(4) *Pistols.* The pistol cannot be recocked or refired without opening the breech. Wait 10 seconds; then retract the slide to extract and eject malfunctioning cartridge.

43. Malfunctions of Weapons

Table III lists the probable causes of malfunctions and corrective measures are indicated.

Table III. Troubleshooting

Malfunction	Probable causes	Corrective action
a. Cal..22 High Standard Automatic Pistol (Supermatic) and Cal..22 Ruger Mark I Automatic Pistol (Target Model) (67/s-In. Barrel).		
Failure to feed................................	Rough chamber or bur on edge of chamber. Sticking firing pin .... Weak driving spring .... Weak magazine spring .... Broken magazine catch .... Battered cartridge	Notify unit gunsmith. Remove cartridge (par. 20c or 21e).
	Dirt in magazine assembly .... Dirty magazine catch	Clean magazine (par. 38) Clean weapon (par. 38).
Failure to load	Cartridge not extracted .... Dirty chamber	Notify unit gunsmith. Clean chamber (par. 38).
Failure to fire	Detective primer .... Broken firing pin................................... Weak driving spring .... Defective sear or hammer .... Short firing pin .... Firing pin hole in slide off location giving impression of firing pin otf rim of cartridge.	Discard cartridge (par. 20c). Notify unit gunsmith.

AGO 10003A

Table III. Troubleshooting-Continued

Malfunction	Probable causes	Corrective action
Failure to function freely	Slide binding due to burs from-	
	Hammer rebound	
	Sear bar rebound	Remove burs.
	Slide lock contact	
	Slide binds in frame, as a result of attempt to remove slide side play by squeezing slide in vise.	To eliminate drag in the slide when it is on the frame, tap slide with a plastic hammer.
	Lack of lubrication	Lubricate (par. 36).
b. Cal 38 Special Smith and Wesson Revolver K-38 (Masterpiece).		
Failure to feed	Dirty cylinder	Clean cylinder (par. 38).
	Battered cartridge	Remove cartridge (par. 22c).
Failure of cylinder to rotate	Broken thumb piece or hand	Notify unit gunsmith.
	Dirt or obstruction on chamber	Clean weapon (par. 38).
Failure to fire	Broken mainspring	Notify unit gunsmith.
	Defective primer	Remove cartridge (par. 22).
	Broken hammer	Notify unit gunsmith.
c. Cal 22 M12 and Cal 30-06 Rifles.		
Failure to feed	Weak magazine spring	Notify unit gunsmith.
	Battered cartridge	Remove cartridge (par. 25).
Failure to extract	Broken extractor	Notify unit gunsmith.
	Dirt in chamber	Clean chamber (par. 38).
Failure to fire	Broken firing pin	
	Broken sear	Notify unit gunsmith.
	Deformed spring	
	Defective primer	Remove cartridge (par. 25).

Section IV. FIELD STRIPPING

44. General

Field stripping is the disassembly of a weapon into its subassemblies. Field stripping may be performed as a function of preventive maintenance when required to inspect parts for wear or damage.

45. Cal..22 High Standard Automatic Pistol (Supermatic)

 a. Removal of Subassemblies.

 (1) Depress magazine catch and remove magazine assembly (par. 10a).

 (2) Operate slide assembly (par. 10h), and unload any cartridge remaining in the chamber.

 (3) Move safety lever to SAFE position (par. 10b).

 (4) Depress the barrel plunger (par. 10f) and slide the barrel (fig. 46) off the front of the frame.

 (5) Release the safety lever (par. 10b).

 (6) Remove the slide assembly from the front of the frame.

 b. Installation of Subassemblies.

 (1) Install slide assembly from front of frame by aligning with grooves on frame.

 (2) Depress barrel plunger (par. 10f) and slide barrel on the frame and press

AGO 10003A

on the barrel until plunger locks the cam into position.
(3) Push safety lever to SAFE position (par. 10b).
(4) Insert magazine assembly into frame.

46. Cal 22 Ruger Mark I Automatic Pistol (Target Model) (67/s-In. Barrel)

a. Removal of Subassemblies.
(1) Depress magazine catch and remove the magazine assembly (fig. 19) (par. 11b).
(2) Remove any cartridge remaining in the chamber (par. 11c).
(3) Pull the housing latch out to release the mainspring housing assembly (fig. 47) from the grip frame. Rotate the mainspring housing about the bolt stop pin pivot until the claw on the housing is released from the receiver. Withdraw the bolt stop pin from the grip frame, receiver, and bolt, and remove housing and pin.
(4) Slide the bolt assembly from the receiver.
(5) Slide the barrel and receiver forward on grip frame to release the frame from the receiver.

b. Installation of Subassemblies.
(1) Slide the grip frame (fig. 48) onto receiver and barrel assembly. The lug on the frame should fit beneath the slot on the receiver. The final position of front of frame should align with the front of the receiver.
(2) Insert the bolt assembly into the receiver with the recoil spring up. The hammer (L, fig. 57) should be in the cocked position when inserting the bolt assembly.
(3) Press the trigger and with a small screwdriver push the hammer into the released position.
(4) Insert the bolt stop pin into the hole in the grip frame and the slot in the bolt assembly. The pin- should be forced past the recoil spring guide.
(5) Rotate the mainspring housing assembly (fig. 47) about the bolt stop pin, pivot until the claw on the housing engages the receiver.
(6) When folding the mainspring housing assembly into group frame, the ham

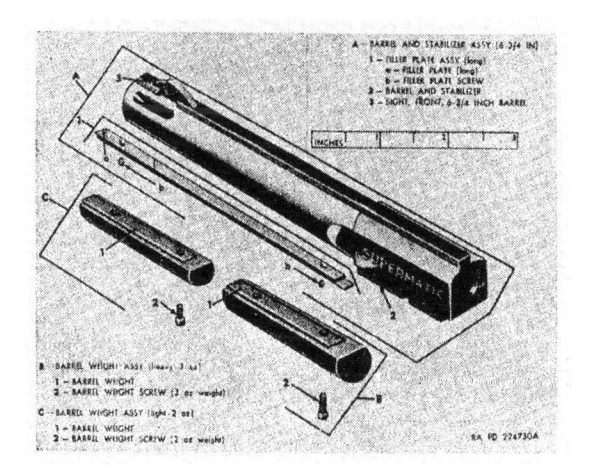

Figure 46. Barrel group-exploded view (high standard).

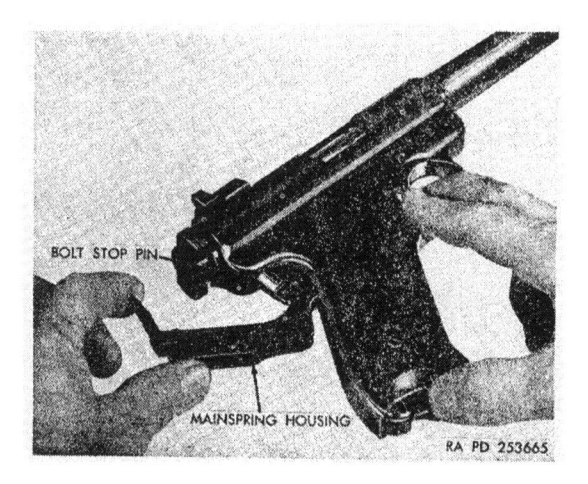

Figure 47. Removing mainspring housing (Ruger).

mer strut should fit into the cupped well on the housing.
(7) Insert housing latch end into the grip frame slot and fold the latch into the housing.
(8) Insert the magazine assembly into the well of the frame.

47. Cal 38 Special, Smith and Wesson Revolver K-38 (Masterpiece)

a. *Removal of Subassemblies.*
(1) Remove side plate forward screws, using screwdriver SW-5193 (fig. 41).
(2) Press forward on thumb piece to release the cylinder assembly (S, fig. 58) and push cylinder assembly to the left.
(3) Slide yoke (Z, fig. 58) and cylinder assembly forward and separate these two components by pulling yoke forward off cylinder assembly.
(4) Remove rear side plate screws from side plate and remove side plate.

b. *Installation of Subassemblies.*
(1) Install side plate and secure with two rear side plate screws.

(2) Assemble yoke assembly to the cylinder group and install as a unit in the frame. Install forward side plate screw to hold the yoke assembly.

48. Cal 22 Rifle M12 (Winchester M52 Heavy Barrel)

a. *Removal of Subassemblies.*
(1) Extract cartridge from chamber (par. 13a(3)).
(2) Press in on the magazine release plunger, located on the right side of the stock, and remove magazine from its opening in the bottom of the stock. Unload cartridges.
(3) Move the safety lever forward to FIRE position, and rotate the breech bolt handle up and draw bolt assembly back as far as it will go. Depress the trigger and pull bolt assembly out of receiver.
(4) Unscrew two receiver base mounting screws holding receiver extension rear sight assembly to the left rear side of the receiver mount and remove sight.
(5) Remove the sling M1907 7141245.
(6) Remove the stock screw from hole just forward of the trigger guard.

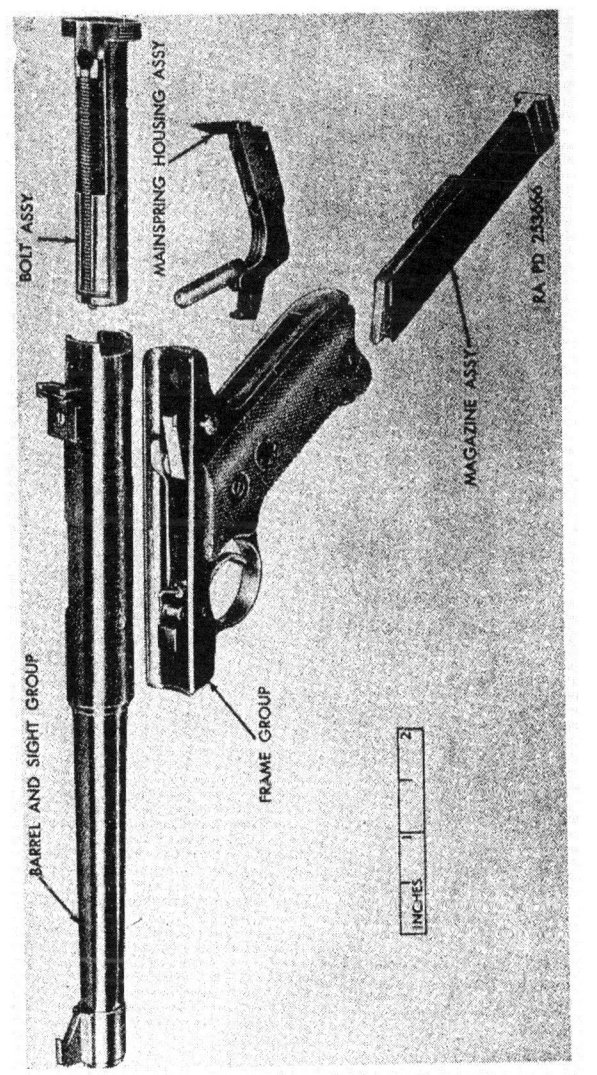

Figure 48. Pistol field stripped (Ruger).

(7) Remove barrel band screw from hole located in line with barrel band on right side of stock.
(8) Remove the tang screw from its hole located in line with the sight and on top of the receiver, and lift the barrel and receiver from the stock as a unit.

b. *Installation of Subassemblies.*
(1) Insert magazine release plunger with its larger diameter to the left through the opening in the middle of the stock and push the plunger all the way to the right.
(2) Place the barrel and receiver group in its opening in the stock with its holes in the rear and front of the receiver and the hole in the barrel band aligned with those in the stock.

Caution: **Before seating the barrel and receiver group, compress the protruding end of the magazine catch to the left until it is flush with the side of the magazine holder. The sharp bottom end of the magazine catch will damage the wooden stock, if the catch is not completely compressed.**

(3) Insert tang screw (fig. 49) through the rear hole of the receiver and into the stock and tighten the screw.
(4) Insert the barrel band screw through the stock and barrel band and tighten it.
(5) Insert stock screw from the bottom of the stock and through the front trigger guard hole and the stock and into the threaded hole in the front of the receiver. Tighten the screw.
(6) Place the receiver extension rear sight assembly (fig. 49) on the left rear side of the receiver with the concave side of the rear sight receiver base to the right and the rear sight disk to the rear. Align holes in receiver base and receiver mount and secure with two base mounting screws.
(7) Install the sling M1907 7141245.
(8) Hold convex side of magazine to the rear and magazine base down and slide the magazine into its recess until it seats and is locked in position (fig. 64).
(9) With the firing pin in the cocked position, slide the breech bolt assembly through the machined groove in the rear end of the receiver as far forward as it will go (fig. 62).
(10) Depress the trigger and push the breech bolt assembly forward of the breech bolt handle locking plunger and the rear, but not all the way forward.
(11) Release the trigger and move the safety to the SAFE position, slide the breech bolt to its foremost position, and lower the breech bolt handle to the locked position.

49. **Cal 22 Rifle M12 (Remington Model M40XS1)**
a. *Removal of Subassemblies.*
(1) Extract cartridge from chamber (par. 13a (3)).
(2) Press up on the bolt stop release located forward of the trigger.
(3) Pull the bolt out the rear opening of the receiver.
(4) Using the screwdriver 5564038 (fig. 43) unscrew the two receiver sight base mounting screws which secure the receiver rear sight assembly to the base, and remove the sight assembly.
(5) Unscrew the front, center, and rear screws from the trigger guard (fig. 50), all of which have clearance holes through the guard, and stock and tapped holes in the bottom of the receiver. Then remove trigger guard, trigger guide plate, and barrel and receiver from stock.

b. *Installation of Subassemblies.*
(1) Place the barrel and receiver group in its seat in the top of the stock (fig. 49). Install trigger guide plate over trigger opening in stock. Align the three trigger guard holes in the stock and receiver (fig. 70). Also align the holes in the top of the stock for the trigger housing assembly and the barrel bracket to receive these two projecting components.

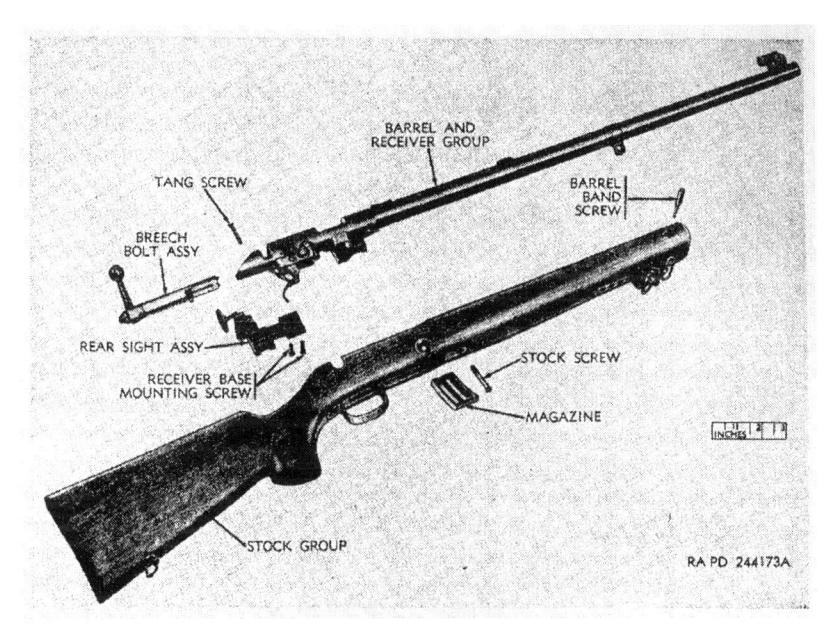

Figure 49. Cal.22 rifle (Winchester M52 heavy barrel) -field stripped.

(2) Install the trigger guide plate and trigger guard in position and insert the front, center, and the rear guard screws in their holes at bottom of stock; push the screws up through the clearance holes in the stock and tighten screws with screwdriver 5564038 (fig. 43).

(3) Place the receiver rear sight assembly on the sight base on the left-rear face of the receiver with the two clearance holes in the base aligned with the two tapped holes on the receiver sight.

(4) Install two receiver sight base mounting screws and tighten.

(5) Install the sling M1 6544058.

(6) If the firing pin in the bolt assembly is not cocked, hold the bolt head stationary by placing it between copper jaws in a vise and rotate bolt handle 66-90 degrees in a counterclockwise direction. This movement will push and hold the firing pin to the rear against the compressed spring.

(7) Align the extractors and the bolt stop locking surface on the bottom of the bolt plug with their respective guide ways and slots in the bolt hole in the rear of the receiver.

(8) With the safety in FIRE position, slide the positioned bolt assembly into the rear opening of the receiver half way.

(9) Depress the bolt stop release, and slide the bolt to its forward position and rotate bolt handle down against the right side of the receiver.

(10) Rotate the safety to the rear in its SAFE position to lock both the bolt and the trigger.

AGO 10003A

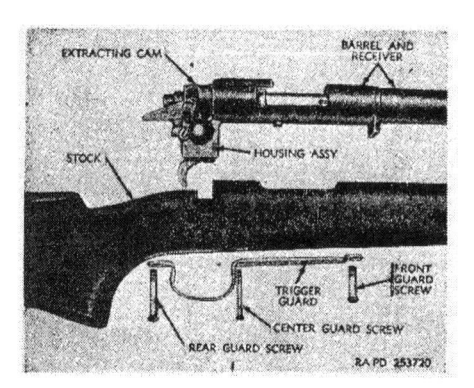

Figure 50. Cal 22 rifle M12 (Remington model 40XS1)-partially field stripped.

50. Cal 30-06 Winchester Rifle Model 70 (Special Match Grade)

a. Removal of Subassemblies.
  (1) Unload cartridges from magazine and chamber (par. 25).
  (2) Remove the bolt assembly (C, fig. 51) (par. 15).
  (3) Remove the Lyman rear sight No. 48WH slide group (par. 16g).
  (4) Remove the Lyman front sight No. 77 from its base (par. 17h).
  (5) Remove the sling-WRA-13170. Depress the magazine cover catch and open the magazine cover. Unscrew magazine cover hinge plate screw and remove cover. Slide magazine spring from magazine cover and magazine follower.
  (6) Remove the guard bow front screw and guard bow rear screw from the stock. Remove the guard bow. Remove the magazine tube from the receiver well.
  (7) Remove the barrel stock screw from the barrel and separate the barrel and receiver group from the stock assembly.

b. Installation of Subassemblies.
  (1) Insert the barrel and receiver in the stock assembly. Screw the barrel stock screw into the barrel.
  (2) Insert the magazine tube into the receiver well. Place the guard bow on the stock and install the guard bow front and rear screws.
  (3) Slide the magazine spring into magazine cover. Slide magazine follower on the spring. Place cover group on the magazine tube and install the magazine cover hinge plate screw into the stock. Install the sling WRA-13170.
  (4) Install Lyman front sight No. 77 on its base (par. 17c).
  (5) Install Lyman rear sight No. 48WH slide group (par. 16).
  (6) Install the bolt assembly (par. 15b).

AGO 10003A

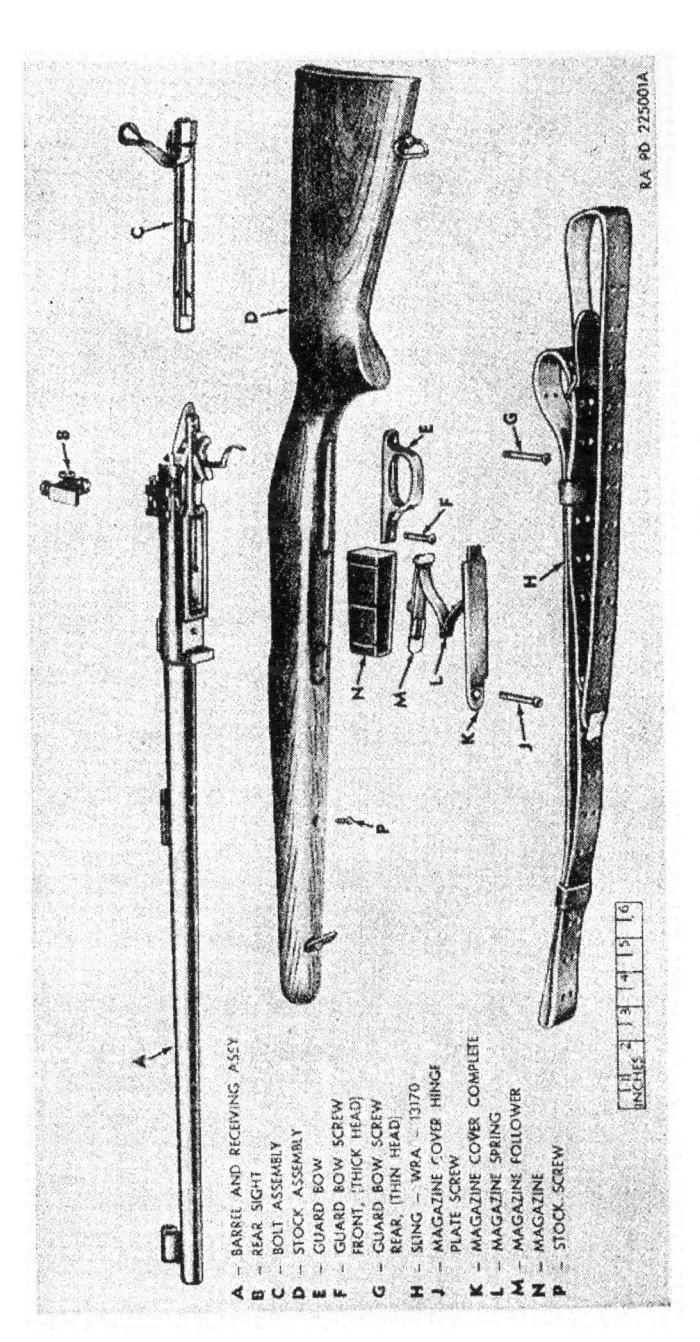

Figure 51. Cal. 30-06 Winchester rifle model 70-field stripped.

CHAPTER 4

MAINTENANCE INSTRUCTIONS

Section I. GENERAL

51. Scope

This chapter contains information and instructions for use by the unit gunsmith.

52. Maintenance Allocation

The publication of these maintenance instructions is not to be construed as authority for the performance by unit gunsmith of these functions that have been restricted to rebuild installations.

Section II. PARTS, SPECIAL TOOLS, AND EQUIPMENT FOR MAINTENANCE

53. General

Tools and equipment available for maintenance are authorized by TA 60-18.

54. Parts

Repair and replacement parts for National Match rifles, pistols and revolvers are listed in SB 9-112, SB 9-125, and SB 9-135. Repairs beyond the scope of the unit gunsmith will be made in accordance with paragraph 33.

55. Common Tools and Equipment

Standard and commonly used tools and equipment having general application to this materiel are listed in SM 9-4-5180-J8-6 and SM 9-4-5180-J10O-2 and are authorized for issue by tables of equipment. They are not specifically identified in this manual.

56. Special Tools and Equipment

Special tools and equipment are authorized in accordance with TA 60-18.

Section III. INSPECTION

57. General

Inspections required for match grade weapons are described in a through g below.

a. Cal 22 High-Standard Automatic Pistol (Supermatic). There are no gage checks required for field inspection of the cal 22 supermatic. Manual cycling, close visual inspection, and function firing will usually suffice to classify the weapon.

(1) Clear the pistol.
(2) Inspect the chamber and bore for obstruction, pitting, rings, or bulges.
(3) Check the rear sight for ease of operation and ability to retain setting.
(4) Check the slide plunger locking action.

Slide and trunnion shall lock tight.
(5) Check the magazine catch for positive retention and release of the magazine.
(6) Check the magazine for burred or deformed lips, bent follower or body, and weak or deformed spring.
(7) Safety shall be positive in the ON and OFF position.
(8) Trigger pull limits are 21/2 pounds minimum and 3 pounds maximum.
(9) After repair, the pistol is function fired 10 rounds to note general opera-

tion and performance of the pistol and magazine.
(10) Immediately after function firing, the pistol shall be fired 5 consecutive rounds at 15 yards with the sights aligned at 6 o'clock on a 3-inch bull's eye. The five shots must fall within the bull's-eye (bench rest).
(11) At the range of 15 yards, 5 consecutive rounds shall fall within or cut a 1inch circle within the bull's-eye (bench rest).
(12) Pistols which do not meet requirements will be turned in.

b. *Cal 22 Ruger Mark I Automatic Pistol.* There are no gage checks required for field inspection of the cal 22 Ruger pistol. Manual cycling, close visual inspection, and function firing will usually suffice to classify the weapon.
(1) Clear the pistol.
(2) Inspect the chamber and bore for obstructions, pitting, rings, or bulges.
(3) Manually cycle the weapon to note general performance and operation.
(4) Check the rear sight for ease of operation and ability to retain setting.
(5) Trigger pull shall be smooth, free from creep, and within the limits of 21/4 pounds minimum to 31/4 pounds maximum.
(6) After assembling, the pistol is function fired nine rounds to note general operation and performance of the pistol and magazine.
(7) Immediately after function firing, the pistol shall be fired 5 consecutive rounds at 15 yards with the sights aligned at 6 o'clock on a 3-inch bull's eye. The five shots must fall within the bull's-eye (bench rest).
(8) At the range of 15 yards, 5 consecutive rounds must fall within or cut a 1-inch circle within the bull's-eye (bench rest).
(9) Pistols which do not meet requirements will be turned in for repair or rebuild.

c. *Cal 38 Special, Smith and Wesson, Model K--8 Revolver.*
(1) The checks listed in (a) through (g) below are recommended only as a guide; sequence of operation is left to the discretion of the inspector after the revolver has been cleared.
(a) Clear the weapon.

(b) Check the six cylinder chambers and the bore of the barrel for obstructions, pitting, fouling, and bulges.
(c) Cycle the revolver, both single and double action, to note performance and operations.
(d) Check-the rear sight to assure ease of adjustment and positive sight setting retention.
(e) Headspace of the K-38 revolver is 0.062 to 0.064 inch and is measured with a flat plug or feeler gage between the rear of the cylinder and the opposing face of the frame.
(f) Clearance between the forward face of the cylinder and the breech face of the barrel should not exceed 0.005 inch as determined by a feeler gage.
(g) Disassembly of the K-38 revolver should be restricted to those parts requiring replacement or deburring.
(2) After assembling, check the trigger pull, headspace, and barrel clearance. Trigger pull limits are 23/1 pounds minimum to 31/2 pounds maximum for single action, and 10 to 12 pounds double action. Check the trigger pull on each chamber.
(a) Function fire six shots to note general performance.
(b) Fire 6 shots for accuracy at 25 yards on a 4-inch bull's-eye. Set rear sight up five clicks for individual adjustment. Fire three shots single action and three shots double action, using a bench rest. Shot pattern shall group within a 1 1/2-inch circle.

d. *Cal 22 Rifle M12.*
(1) Cal 22 rifle M12 (Winchester Model 52). Stocks, trigger mechanisms, and bolts of the Model 52B and Model 52C are not interchangeable. Trigger pull adjustment on the Model 52C may be made by turning the two screws (located ahead of the

AGO 10003A

trigger guard) marked PULL and O. T. (over travel).The bolt must be removed from the Model 52B to gain access to the adjustment screw.

Note. **Lubricants will not be used on the Model 52C trigger housing or components, as these parts have been carefully machined to close tolerances, honed, and hard chrome plated. Use carbon tetrachloride to remove lubricants that may accidentally get into the trigger mechanism.**

(a) Inspection of the Winchester rifle Model 52 is limited to visual inspection, except for headspace gaging, which may be accomplished with standard ordnance gages.

(b) Clear the rifle.

(c) Inspect the bore and chamber for obstructions.

(d) Check rear sight for elevation, windage adjustment, and ability to retain setting.

(e) The barrel and action are bedded on rubber. Care must be exercised to assure that these strips are assembled and positioned properly.

(f) Disassembly of the bolt and trigger groups will be accomplished only when repairs are necessary.

(g) Prescribed trigger pull is 3 pounds minimum and 4 pounds maximum. Trigger pull and/or linear over-travel may be adjusted by turning the adjustment screws.

(h) After assembly, the rifle should be fired for accuracy at a range of 100 yards, using a rest. Extreme spread for 10 consecutive shots should not exceed 2 inches.

(2) Cal 22 rifle M12 (Remington Model 40X-S1). Data for this weapon will be furnished as it becomes available.

e. *Winchester Rifle Model 70.* Inspection of the cal 30-06 Winchester rifle Model 70.

(1) Clear the rifle.

(2) Inspect the bore and chamber for obstructions.

(3) Firing pin protrusion is 0.058 to 0.068 inch. Headspace: minimum 1.942 inches, maximum 1.945 inches.

(4) Check front and rear sights for deformation, burs, or looseness.

(5) After assembly, the rifle shall be hand cycled to note general performance.

(6) Trigger pull is 3 pounds minimum and 3 1/2 pounds maximum. Adjustment is effected by moving the trigger spring adjustment nuts down or up to obtain the desired pull. After adjustment is obtained, the mechanism is locked by turning the nut nearest the worker down onto the other nut.

(7) At the range of 100 yards, using a bench rest, the Model 70 Winchester shall group 5 shots within or cutting a 1-inch circle.

58. Troubleshooting

a. It is important that the weapon and all its equipment be properly installed and maintained. Proper care of the weapons and proper preventive maintenance will greatly reduce the possibility of stoppage due to malfunction of the materiel.

b. Most malfunctions fall into categories listed in table IV.

Table IV. Troubleshooting

Malfunction	Probable causes	Corrective action
a. Cal 22 High Standard Automatic Pistol (Supermatic) and Cal 22 Ruger Mark I Automatic Pistol' (Target Model) (67/-In. Barrel). Failure to feed	Sticking firing pin	Ream firing pin hole with 1/8-inch drill (par. 61c).
	Weak driving spring (High Standard) or recoil spring assembly (Ruger).	Replace driving spring (par. 61) or recoil spring assembly (par. 67).

Table IV. Troubleshooting-Continued

Malfunction	Probable causes	Corrective action
	Weak magazine spring	Replace magazine spring (par. 62 or 68).
	Broken magazine catch	Replace magazine catch (par. 63 or 69).
	Chamber rough or bur on chamber edge (caused by long firing pin hitting chamber).	Replace barrel (par. 45).
Failure to load	Cartridge not extracted due to broken extractor.	Replace extractor (par. 61 or 67).
	Cartridge not extracted due to weak extractor spring.	Replace extractor spring (par. 61 or 67).
Failure to fire	Short firing pin	Replace pin (par. 61 or 67).
	Broken firing pin	
	Weak driving spring (High Standard) or recoil spring assembly.	Replace driving spring (par. 61) or 67. recoil spring assembly (par. 67).
	Worn or broken sear	Stone or replace sear (par. 63 or 69).
	Worn hammer	Stone or replace hammer (par. 63 or 69).
	Firing pin hole in slide off location giving impression of firing pin off rim of cartridge.	Replace slide assembly (par. 45).
b. Cal 38 Special Smith and Wesson Revolver K-38 (Masterpiece).		
Failure to feed	Deformed cylinder assembly	Replace cylinder assembly (par. 47b).
Failure of cylinder to rotate	Broken bolt	Replace bolt (par. 70).
	Worn thumb piece	Replace thumb piece (par. 70).
	Broken hand	Replace hand (par. 70).
Failure to fire	Broken or weak mainspring	Replace mainspring (par. 70).
	Broken hammer	Replace hammer (par. 70).
c. Cal 22 Rifle M12 and Cal 30-06 Winchester Rifle Model 70 (Special Match Grade).		
Failure to feed	Weak magazine spring	Replace magazine spring (par. 84).
Failure to load	Cartridge not extracted-broken extractor.	Replace extractor (par. 81).
Failure to fire	Broken or worn firing pin	Replace firing pin (par. 63).
	Broken or worn sear	Replace sear (par. 84).

Section IV. CAL 22 HIGH-STANDARD AUTOMATIC PISTOL (SUPERMATIC)

59. Removal and Installation of Subassemblies

a. See paragraph 45a for breakdown of weapon into barrel assembly, slide assembly, frame group, and magazine assembly.

b. See paragraph 45b for installation of subassemblies.

60. Barrel Assembly

a. Disassembly. Disassembly of the barrel assembly will be limited to removal of barrel weights as described in paragraph 10d.

b. Maintenance.

(1) See paragraph 38 for cleaning instructions and paragraph 36 for lubrication instructions of the bore and chamber.

(2) Inspect the bore for pitting and sharpness of lands. Pitting less than width

of a land or groove and less than 1/8 inch long is acceptable.

  c. *Assembly.* See paragraph 10ad for assembly of barrel weights or filler plate to the barrel assembly.

61. Slide Assembly

  a. *General.* The slide assembly (A) consists mainly of the driving spring group, adjustable rear sight assembly (B), extractor group, and firing pin group.

  Note. The key letters shown below in parentheses refer to figure 52.

  b. *Disassembly.*

  (1) Drive out the driving spring plug pin (A-6), and remove the driving spring plug (A-1) driving spring (A-2), and driving spring plunger (A-3) from the slide (A-10).

  (2) Drive out the extractor plunger retaining pin (A-7). Depress the extractor plunger (A-4) to the rear of the slide (A-10). While holding plunger, remove the extractor (A-8) from slot in the slide. Allow extractor spring (A-5) pressure to be released slowly and remove plunger and spring from the well in the slide.

  (3) Drive out firing pin retaining pin (A-9), and remove firing pin (A-lid), rear sleeve (A-11b), center (nylon) sleeve (A-11a), and front sleeve (A-11c).

  (4) Unscrew and remove the rear sight elevation screw (B-3). Place a shim under the rear sight spring (B-5) to prevent marring of the slide finish.
  Drive out the rear sight retaining pin (B-1)Drive the base (B-6) and leaf group over the shim and off the slide (A-10). Remove the spring from the slide. Unscrew the windage screw (B-2) from the rear sight leaf (B-4) and remove leaf from rear sight base.

  c. *Maintenance.*

  (1) Inspect firing pin (A-lid) for mushrooming. It should protrude approximately three-quarters of the way from the shoulder to front of the slide.
  Stone shoulder on pin, if pin does not protrude sufficiently. Ream firing pin AGO 10003A hole to 1/8 inch if required. Replace worn firing pins. Replace a broken nylon sleeve (A-11a).

  (2) The driving spring (A-2) tension should be great enough to return slide to battery. Replace a set or kinked spring.

  (3) Inspect extractor (A-8) for deformation; replace, if necessary. Check tension in extractor spring (A-5); replace if kinked or set.

  (4) If rear sight leaf (B-4) is bent, remove the sight elevation screw from assembled sight and insert a wedge beneath leaf. Straighten leaf carefully with a mallet. Check rear sight spring for tension; replace if necessary.

  (5) The central rib of the slide may be burred from striking surface of hammer. Remove burs carefully with a fine stone.

  d. *Assembly.*

  (1) Insert the adjustable rear sight leaf (B-4) onto the adjustable rear sight base (B-6). Screw in the adjustable rear sight windage screw (B-2) into base and leaf, aligning groove in screw with the pin hole in the base.

  (2) Place adjustable rear sight spring (B-5) under adjustable rear sight base (B-6) and with a shim placed on slide (A-10), to prevent marring slide, drive base (B-6) into a slot on slide. Align pin hole in base with hole in slide and drive in adjustable rear sight retaining pin (B-1). Screw in the adjustable rear sight elevator, screw (B-3).

  (3) Insert front firing pin sleeve (A-11c) which is convex, center firing pin sleeve (A-11c) which is a nylon sleeve, and rear firing pin sleeve (A11b) into the well on the slide. Insert the firing pin through the three sleeves into well and drive in the firing pin retaining pin (A-9).

  (4) Insert the extractor spring (A-5)1 and extractor plunger (A-4) into the well in slide (A-10). Depress the plunger and insert the extractor (A-8') into

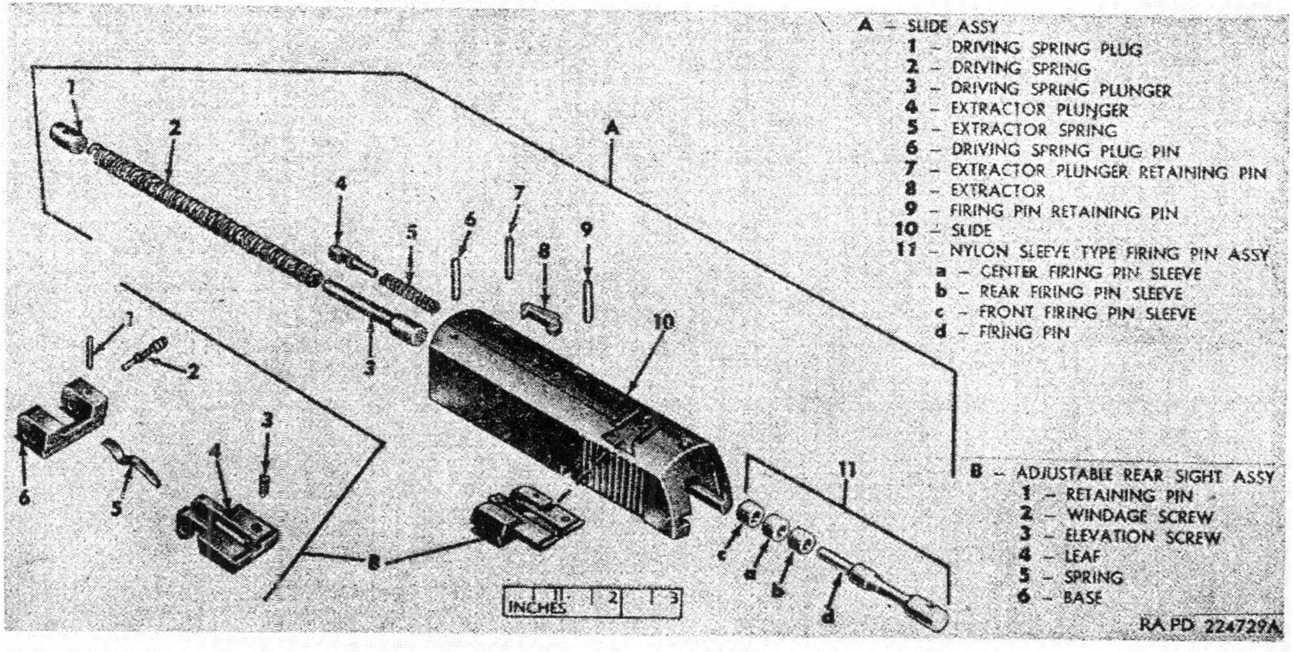

A – SLIDE ASSY
1 – DRIVING SPRING PLUG
2 – DRIVING SPRING
3 – DRIVING SPRING PLUNGER
4 – EXTRACTOR PLUNGER
5 – EXTRACTOR SPRING
6 – DRIVING SPRING PLUG PIN
7 – EXTRACTOR PLUNGER RETAINING PIN
8 – EXTRACTOR
9 – FIRING PIN RETAINING PIN
10 – SLIDE
11 – NYLON SLEEVE TYPE FIRING PIN ASSY
a – CENTER FIRING PIN SLEEVE
b – REAR FIRING PIN SLEEVE
c – FRONT FIRING PIN SLEEVE
d – FIRING PIN

B – ADJUSTABLE REAR SIGHT ASSY
1 – RETAINING PIN
2 – WINDAGE SCREW
3 – ELEVATION SCREW
4 – LEAF
5 – SPRING
6 – BASE

RA PD 224729A

Figure 52. Slide assembly-exploded view (high standard).

the slot in the front of the slide. Allow spring pressure to be released, so that plunger overrides the extractor. Drive in the extractor plunger retaining pin (A-7)

(5) Insert the driving spring plunger (A-3), driving spring (A-2), and plunger spring plug (A-1) into well in slide (A-10). Depress spring and drive in driving spring plug pin (A-6).

62. Magazine Assembly

a. General. The magazine assembly (fig. 53) consists of the magazine tube, magazine follower, magazine button, and magazine spring.

b. Disassembly. Depress magazine follower and remove the magazine button from enlarged slot in magazine tube. Remove follower and magazine spring from front of tube.

c. Maintenance. Remove dents from magazine tube. Check spacing of lips on the front of tube for tightest fit of cartridge. Replace worn magazine spring, magazine follower, or follower button.

d. Assembly. Insert magazine spring and magazine follower into magazine tube. Depress spring and insert magazine button into hole in follower.

63. Frame Group

Note. The key letters shown below in parentheses refer to figure 54.

a. General. The frame group (fig. 54) consists mainly of the grip group, barrel plunger group, and trigger group.

b. Disassembly.

(1) Unscrew the grip screw (A) from the grip screw nut (Z) and remove the two grips (B).

(2) Drive out the magazine catch pin (CC). Remove magazine catch (BB) and the magazine catch spring (AA).

(3) Remove the slide lock lever (X) and slide lock spring (W). Separate spring and lever only if replacement of either part is required.

(4) Unscrew the side plate screw (C) and remove the side plate (D). Remove the safety lever (HH) from the frame. Pull the sear bar spring (E) from the slot in frame and remove the sear bar (F).

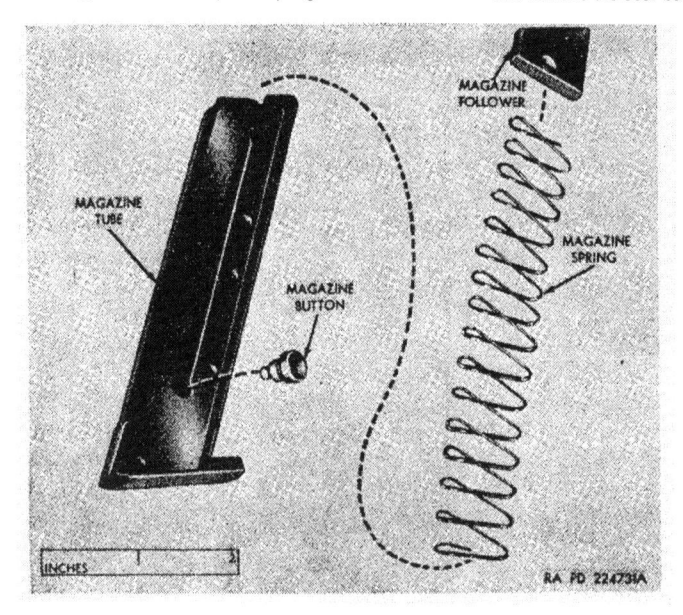

Figure 53. Magazine assembly-exploded view (high standard).

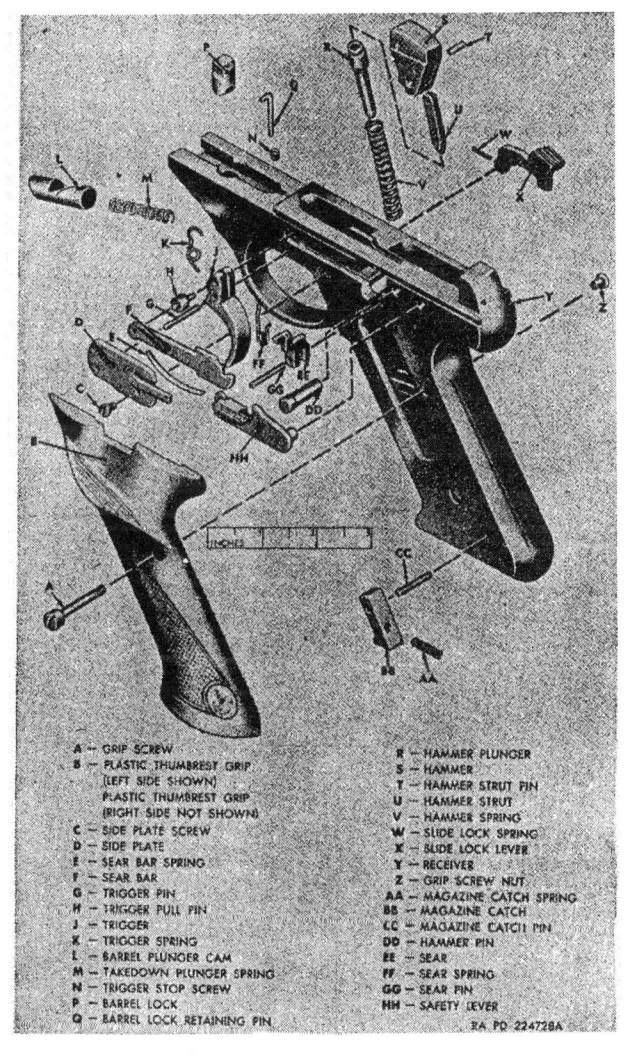

Figure 54. Frame group-exploded view (high standard).

(5) Drive out the trigger pull pin (H) from the right side of frame. Unscrew the trigger stop screw (N). Drive out the trigger pin (G) from the right side of frame and carefully remove trigger (J) and trigger spring (K) from the top of frame. Separate spring and trigger.

(6) Cock the hammer (S) and hold hammer spring (V) down by inserting drift in test hole in side of frame. Drive out hammer pin (DD) and remove hammer from top of

AGO 10003A 66

frame. Remove drift from test hole.
(7) Remove hammer spring (V) and hammer plunger (R) from well in frame.
(8) Drive out sear pin (GG). Remove sear (EE) and sear spring (FF) from well in side of frame.
(9) The barrel lock retaining pin (Q) is staked into the frame. Pry pin loose and pull pin out towards the front of the frame. Remove barrel lock (P) from top of the frame. Remove barrel plunger cam (L) and takedown plunger spring (M) from well above trigger guard.
(10) Drive out hammer strut pin (T) and remove hammer strut (U).

c. *Maintenance.*
(1) If necessary to adjust dead travel of trigger (J), carefully stone the slot on the sear bar (F) which engages the sear. Replace bent or worn sear bar or sear. Check trigger pull using weights. The trigger should not release with a 2 1/4-pound weight and should release with a 3-pound weight.
(2) Check sear spring (FF) and trigger spring (K) for bending, deformation, and set; replace if necessary.
(3) Smooth the striking surface of hammer (S), if burs occur on the slide rib. Replace hammer if excessively worn.
(4) Peen pin on safety lever (HH) if loose; replace the lever if bent or broken. Lever must be fitted to the sear.
(5) Inspect camming surfaces on barrel plunger cam (L) and barrel lock (P) for excessive wear; replace, if necessary. Replace set or kinked plunger spring (M).
(6) Replace weak or kinked magazine catch springs (AA). Replace broken magazine catch (BB). Replace broken or set hammer spring (V).

d. *Assembly.*
(1) Insert takedown plunger spring (M) and barrel plunger cam (L) into well above trigger guard. Insert barrel lock (P) into well in top of frame. Depress lock and insert barrel lock retaining pin (Q) into slot in frame. Stake frame to pin in two places.
(2) To install sear (EE) and sear spring (FF), a short slave pin, the width of the sear, must be used to hold sear spring in place. Insert sear and spring in proper location by holding sear with needle-nose pliers. Using a drift, drive out slave pin. The sear is now in working position. Insert sear pin (GG) into side of frame.
(3) Insert the hammer spring and the hammer plunger (R) in the well in the frame. Depress the plunger and hold in place with a drift in the test hole in the side of frame.
(4) Insert the hammer (S) into the frame alining hammer strut on to the head of the frame plunger. Push hammer pin (DD) into frame and hammer hole. Remove the drift from the test hole.
(5) Insert trigger spring (K) in slot in the trigger (J) and insert them both into frame. Insert trigger pin (G) into frame trigger and trigger spring. Screw in trigger stop screw (N) completely tight. Insert trigger pull pin (H) into frame and trigger.
(6) Insert the sear bar (F) in the slot in the frame, and the sear bar spring (E) beneath the sear bar. Insert the pin on the safety lever (HH) into the pin hole in the frame. Insert the side plate (D) over the bar and the lever and screw in the side plate screw (C). Back off the trigger stop screw until the hammer just releases when the trigger is pulled.
(7) Force narrow end of slide lock spring (W) into well in slide lock lever (X) and insert both into slot on right side of frame.
(8) Insert magazine catch spring (AA) into well in magazine catch (BB) and insert them both into frame. Insert magazine catch pin (CC) into hole in the frame and catch.
(9) Aline left and right thumbrest grips (B) on the frame. Screw in grip screw (A) to grip screw nut (Z).

Section V. CAL. .22 RUGER MARK I AUTOMATIC PISTOL (TARGET MODEL)

64. Removal and Installation of Assemblies.

a. See paragraph 46*a* for breakdown of the weapon, into the barrel and receiver group, bolt assembly, grip frame group, mainspring housing assembly, and magazine assembly.

b. See paragraph 46*b* for installation of subassemblies.

65. Barrel and Receiver Group.

a. Disassembly. Disassembly of the barrel and receiver group will be limited to removal of the rear sight elevation screw (fig. 20) for cleaning.

b. Maintenance.
  (1) See paragraph 38 for cleaning instructions, and paragraph 36 for lubrication instructions.
  (2) Refer to paragraph 60b(2) for bore inspection information.
  (3) Use mineral spirits paint thinner or dry cleaning solvent for cleaning the rear sight hinge springs and sight steadying spring.

c. Assembly. Screw in the rear sight elevation screw and zero the sight as described in paragraph 26.

66. Mainspring Housing Assembly.

a. General. No disassembly of the mainspring housing assembly is authorized.

b. Maintenance.
  (1) Examine mainspring for tension and set.
  (2) Inspect claws on housing for wear.
  (3) Examine housing latch for proper holding to frame.

67. Bolt Assembly.

a. General. The bolt assembly (fig. 55) consists of the recoil spring assembly, firing pin, rebound spring support, rebound spring, firing pin stop, extractor, extractor spring, and extractor plunger.

b. Disassembly.
  (1) Lift off the recoil spring assembly (fig. 55) from the top of the bolt.
  (2) Drive out the firing pin stop, and remove the firing pin, rebound spring support, and rebound spring from the bolt.
  (3) Depress the extractor plunger and, while holding the plunger, remove the extractor. Slowly release pressure on the extractor spring, and remove the plunger and spring.

c. Maintenance.
  (1) Examine the firing pin for mushrooming and replace the pin if necessary.
  (2) Inspect the extractor for wear and burs. Replace broken extractor.

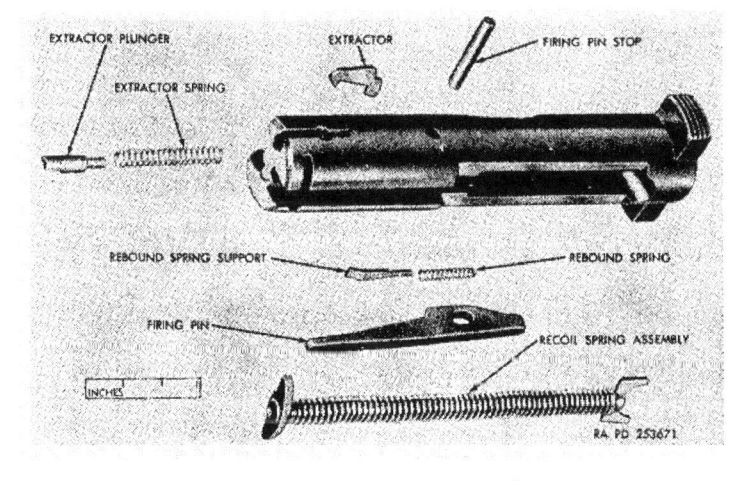

Figure 55. Bolt assembly-exploded view (Ruger).

AGO 10008A

(3) If rebound spring or extractor spring is bent or set, replace spring.
(4) If recoil spring assembly is bent, kinked, or broken, replace the spring assembly.
(5) Stone the front of bolt slightly if cartridges fail to seat properly in the bolt recess.

d. *Assembly.*
(1) Insert extractor spring and plunger into the well of the bolt. Depress plunger and insert extractor into the slot in the bolt. Allow plunger to ride over the lip on the extractor.
(2) Insert rebound spring onto rebound spring support; then insert them both into the slot in the bolt with bent edge of support down.
(3) Insert the firing pin over the support and spring. Aline hole in pin with bolt hole and drive in firing pin stop. Test pin for ease of motion.
(4) Insert recoil spring assembly into slot on the bolt.

68. Magazine Assembly.
a. General. The magazine assembly (fig. 56) consists of the magazine frame, magazine follower, magazine follower button, and the magazine spring.

b. Disassembly. Depress the magazine spring and slide magazine follower back until magazine follower button can be removed from slot in magazine frame. Remove follower and spring from front of frame.

c. Maintenance.
(1) Inspect magazine spring for set or kinks; replace if necessary.
(2) Remove burs from magazine follower and magazine follower button; replace if worn or broken.

d. Assembly. Insert magazine spring and magazine follower into magazine frame. Hold back on spring and insert magazine follower button into hole in magazine follower.

69. Grip Frame Group.
Note. **The key letters shown below in parentheses refer to figure 55.**

a. General. The grip frame group (fig. 57) consists mainly of the trigger group, hammer and sear group, and magazine catch group.

b. Disassembly.
(1) Remove grip screw (B), left hand grip (A), and right hand grip. Push out hammer pivot pin (J) and remove the hammer (L), hammer bushing (K), and safety catch (P). Separate the bushing and hammer.
(2) Remove the trigger pin lockwasher (D) from inside the frame (H).
(3) Push out the trigger pivot pin (C), and remove the trigger (Y) and disconnector (G) group.
(4) Remove the trigger spring plunger (E) and trigger spring (F) from the trigger (Y). Separate the disconnector (G) from the trigger.
(5) Push out the sear pivot pin (W) and remove the sear spring (U) and sear (V).
(6) Drive out the magazine catch pivot pin (S) and remove the magazine catch (R). Drive out the magazine catch stop pin (T) and remove the magazine catch spring (Q).
(7) Drill out staking on hammer strut pin (N) and remove pin. Remove hammer strut (M) from hammer.
(8) Drive out sear spring stop pin (X).

c. Maintenance.
(1) Inspect hammer (L) and sear for worn notches; replace if necessary. If trigger pull is heavy or light, proper stoning of notch on hammer with a fine grit triangular oilstone can adjust the pull. To make trigger pull heavier, stone the hammer notch to .^ positive angle (hook). To make the trigger pull lighter, stone the hammer notch to a negative angle (upsweep). The pull should always remain between 40 and 50 ounces. Replace bent or worn sear spring (U).
(2) Inspect the safety catch (P) for wear in notches or bending; replace if necessary. If safety catch moves sluggishly, the safety catch notch may be lightly stoned.

69

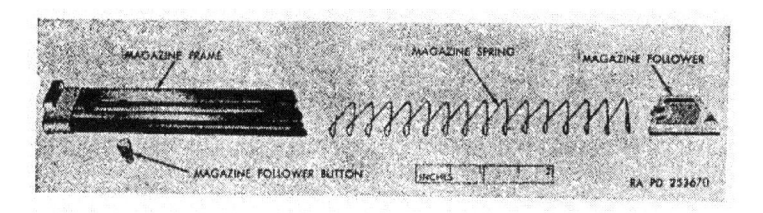

Figure 56. Magazine assembly-exploded view (Ruger).

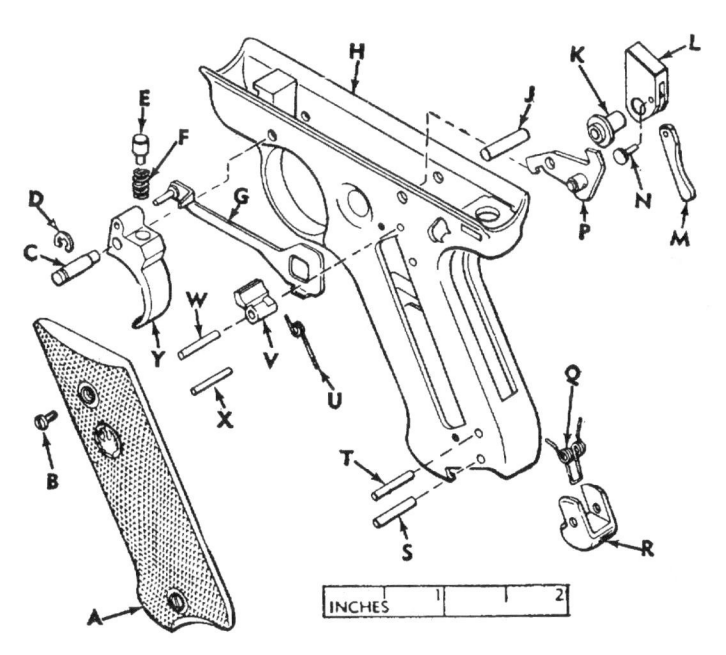

A - LEFT HAND GRIP
B - GRIP SCREW
C - TRIGGER PIVOT PIN
D - TRIGGER PIN LOCK WASHER
E - TRIGGER SPRING PLUNGER
F - TRIGGER SPRING
G - DISCONNECTOR
H - FRAME
J - HAMMER PIVOT PIN
K - HAMMER BUSHING
L - HAMMER
M - HAMMER STRUT

N - HAMMER STRUT PIN
P - SAFETY CATCH
Q - MAGAZINE CATCH SPRING
R - MAGAZINE CATCH
S - MAGAZINE CATCH PIVOT PIN
T - MAGAZINE CATCH STOP PIN
U - SEAR SPRING
V - SEAR
W - SEAR PIVOT PIN
X - SEAR SPRING STOP PIN
Y - TRIGGER

RA PD 253672

Figure 57. Grip frame group--exploded view (Ruger).

(3) Straighten Dent disconnector (G). Replace kinked or set trigger spring (F).
(4) Replace bent or broken hammer strut (N).
(5) Remove burs from magazine catch (R); replace if necessary. Replace worn or bent magazine catch springs (Q).

d. *Assembly.*
(1) Aline hole in hammer (L) and hammer strut (M) and insert hammer strut pin (N). Stake the pin.
(2) Aline magazine catch spring (Q) with hole in frame and insert magazine catch stop pin (T). Aline magazine catch (R) with hole in frame (H) and insert magazine catch pivot pin (S).
(3) Aline hole in sear (V), sear spring (U), and frame (H), and insert sear pivot pin (W) into frame hole through the sear and spring.
(4) Insert the trigger spring (F) and trigger spring plunger (E) into well on trigger. Insert disconnector (G) into hole in trigger. Insert trigger group into frame, and insert trigger pivot pin (C) into hole in frame and trigger (Y). Insert the trigger pin lock washer (D) onto the groove in the pivot pin.
(5) Insert hammer bushing (K) into hole in hammer (L) Insert safety catch (P) into hole in frame (H). Aline hammer with hole in frame, catch, and disconnectors; then insert the hammer pivot pin (J).
(6) Aline left hand grip (A) and right hand grip on frame and screw in the grip screw (B).

Section VI. CAL..38 SPECIAL, SMITH AND WESSON REVOLVER K-38 (MASTERPIECE)

70. Disassembly Note.

Note. The key letters shown below in parentheses refer to figure 58.

a. Remove subassemblies (par. 47).
b. Remove stock screw and stocks (B).
c. Lift out hammer block (CC).
d. Remove strain screw (NN). Depress top end of mainspring (QQ) and disengage stirrup (H) from mainspring hooks. Remove the mainspring.
e. Pull back on thumbpiece and hold it to the rear. Pull hammer group back to the cocked position. With index finger of right hand, hold the trigger (PP) in the rear position and lift hammer group out. Release the trigger.
f. Before attempting to remove rebound slide assembly, carefully lift its rear end away from the frame to clear the rebound slide stud (E), compressing the trigger spring (D) enough to relieve the tension against the rebound .slide stud.

Caution: Relax the spring tension gradually after clearing the stud to prevent loss of, or damage to, the spring.

Remove rebound assembly and rebound slide (F) and trigger spring.

g. Remove trigger group by holding upper end of hand assembly to the rear until it clears the frame. Lift trigger group from trigger post.
h. Separate trigger assembly and hand (KK) by exerting upward pressure on hand spring (MM), using suitable small screwdriver. Remove hand from the trigger. Release tension on hand spring.
i. Remove cylinder stop screw (EE), plunger spring, and cylinder stop plunger (GG). Swing cylinder stop (HH) into downward position and lift out.
j. Remove thumbpiece screw and lift off thumbpiece. Press bolt (M) to rear, lift out rear of bolt upward and out of frame (C), using care not to distort bolt or lose bolt plunger spring and bolt plunger (J) which are in rear end of bolt. Separate spring and plunger from bolt.
k. Remove the locking bolt (W) by driving out locking bolt pin in barrel lug (AA) on underside of barrel. Remove the locking bolt spring (X).
l. Disassemble the hammergroup as outlined in (1) and (2) below.
(1) Drive out the stirrup pin and remove the stirrup (H).

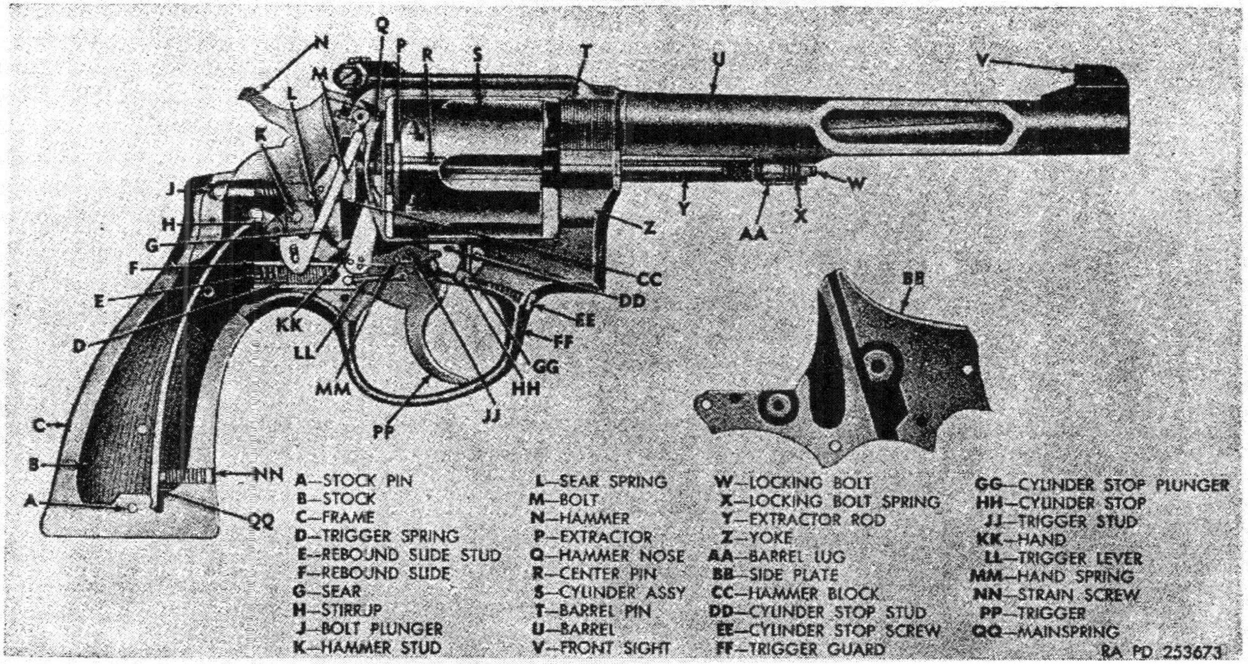

Figure 58. Cal. .38 special Smith and Wesson revolver K–8 (Masterpiece)-cross section view.

(2) Drive out sear pin which secures sear (G) to the hammer (N) and release sear slowly to prevent loss or damage to the sear spring (L).

m. Drive out hand spring pin and remove hand spring (MM). Drive out hand spring torsion pin.

n. Drive out trigger lever pin and remove trigger lever (LL).

71. Inspection and Maintenance.

Note. The key letters shown below in parentheses refer to figure 58.

a. Inspect stock (B) for cracks, deep scars, or any defect which may affect serviceability. Replace stocks on which checkering is worn or smooth. Small cracks or chips, which do not affect the strength of the part, will not be cause for replacement. If unserviceable, replace stock.

b. Inspect the yoke assembly (Z) for alinement, looseness, and wear. Check that yoke number corresponds with number on frame and side plate.

c. Inspect cylinder assembly (S) for burs, pits, and other defects which may affect proper functioning. The cylinder is to be free of corrosion and powder fouling. Pits are allowed in the chambers, if they are not large enough to cause extraction difficulties.

d. Inspect extractor (P) and extractor rod (Y) for alinement, tension of extractor rod spring, and functioning of center pin.

e. Inspect mainspring (QQ) for cracks, burs, or wear. Inspect hooks, which engage the stirrup, for distortion. Replace mainspring if necessary.

f. Check that hammer nose is smooth and well rounded, and make certain that hammer pin hole is not elongated. Replace a worn or broken hammer (N).

g. Inspect trigger (PP) and trigger lever (LL) for wear, cracks, or breakage. Check trigger pull for single action, using test weights of 2 1/2 and 3 1/2 pounds. A 2 1/2 pound weight attached to the trigger should not release the sear, but with a 3 1/2-pound weight attached, the sear should release.

h. Check trigger spring (D) for corrosion and distortion. Replace a worn or broken spring. Replace a broken hand (K).

l. Check bolt plunger (J) and bolt plunger spring for wear or distortion; replace them necessary.

j. Examine thumbpiece, locking bolt (W), locking bolt spring (X), and locking bolt pin for burs, wear, or distortion. Replace them if unserviceable.

k. Inspect barrel for pitting, bulges, and sharpness of lands. Inspect muzzle and breech end for burs. Inspect breech end for erosion caused by gases escaping between the barrel and the cylinder.

72. Assembly.

Note. The key letters shown below in parentheses refer to figure 58.

a. Install locking bolt spring (X) and locking bolt (W) with the flat surface up. Drive locking bolt pin into lug on the underside of barrel.

b. Install cylinder stop (HH) on its pin in the frame. Install cylinder stop plunger (GG), spring, and cylinder stop screw (EE).

c. Install hand spring torsion pin, hand spring (MM), and hand spring pin in the trigger (PP). Using a suitable screwdriver, exert upward pressure on the hand spring and install hand assembly (KK). Insert trigger lever (LL) into trigger and drive in trigger lever pin.

d. Install assembled trigger group on the trigger post, holding upper end of hand assembly to the rear until it clears the frame.

e. Install bolt plunger (J) and bolt plunger spring in recess in rear end of bolt.

f. Install bolt (M) in its recess in the frame by pressing the bolt plunger (J) forward.

g. Position thumbpiece and install the thumbpiece screw.

h. Install stirrup (H) on hammer (N) and drive in stirrup pin. Install sear spring (L) and sear (G) on the hammer and secure them with the sear pin.

I. Install hammer group on hammer post, while holding trigger, and bolt in rearward position.

j. Put trigger spring (D) into the rebound slide (F) after compressing the spring. Install the rebound slide assembly against the retaining pin in the frame, with the leveled end forward, so the rear of the trigger lever is positioned in the blind hole in the forward face of the rebound slide.

k. Install mainspring (QQ) by engaging hooks on its upper end with the hammer stirrup, and then pressing the lower end into its recess in the frame.

l. Install the strain screw (NN) and hammer block (CC).

m. Install the stocks (B) and secure with stock screws. Install side plate, yoke assembly, and cylinder group.

n. Secure yoke assembly with forward side plate screw.

Section VII. CAL. .22 RIFLE M12 (WINCHESTER RIFLE, MODEL 52 (HEAVY BARREL))

73. Removal and Installation of Subassemblies.

a. See paragraph 48a for breakdown of the rifle into breech bolt assembly, magazine, receiver extension rear sight assembly, barrel and receiver group, and stock group.

b. See paragraph 48b for installation of subassemblies.

74. Breech Bolt Assembly.

a. *General.* The breech bolt assembly (fig. 59) consists mainly of the breech bolt and handle, the firing pin, spring, plug and guide pin, the left-hand and right-hand extractors, extractor springs, and pins.

b. *Disassembly.*
  (1) Place the rear shoulder of the firing pin (fig. 59) in a vise between copper jaws, and do not grip the breech bolt handle between the jaws.
  (2) With the breech bolt handle in the uncocked position, one man pulls the breech bolt from the breech bolt handle and firing pin against the tension of the firing pin spring, until the firing pin guide pin is exposed on the rear shoulder of the breech bolt.
  (3) Another man then drifts the firing pin guide pin out of its holes in the breech bolt and firing pin. Removing the guide pin releases the tension of the firing pin spring and separates the firing pin and breech bolt handle from the breech bolt.
  (4) Using the screwdriver 5564038 (fig. 43), unscrew the firing pin plug from its hole in the rear of the firing pin and remove the firing pin spring.
  (5) Drive out the two extractor pins from the bottom toward the top of the bolt, and remove the two extractors and two extractor springs. Be careful that extractor springs do not fly out.

c. *Maintenance.*
  (1) Inspect the firing pin for worn or mushroom end; replace if damaged. Check firing pin spring for kinks or set; replace if unserviceable.
  (2) Inspect the extractors for excessive wear, dents, or burs; replace if unserviceable. Inspect extractor springs for kinks and set; replace if unserviceable.
  (3) Inspect the bolt for burs.
  (4) Inspect threaded parts for wear and broken threads. Repair or replace items.

d. *Assembly.*
  (1) Install the right-hand extractor spring (fig. 59) in its seat in the front of the breech bolt. Compress the spring with the right-hand extractor (hook shaped) until the holes in the extractor and breech bolt are alined; insert extractor pin in holes. Install the lefthand extractor spring (fig. 59) in its seat in the breech bolt; compress the spring with the left-hand extractor (claw shaped) until the holes in the bolt and extractor are alined; install extractor pin in holes. Extractor pins must not protrude from breech bolt.
  (2) Place the breech bolt in a vise, between copper jaws, with the small end protruding. Slide the breech bolt handle over the small end of the breech bolt.
  (3) Slide the firing pin spring into its seat in the firing pin, and insert the firing pin with the striker end leading, and the flat surface

AGO 10003A

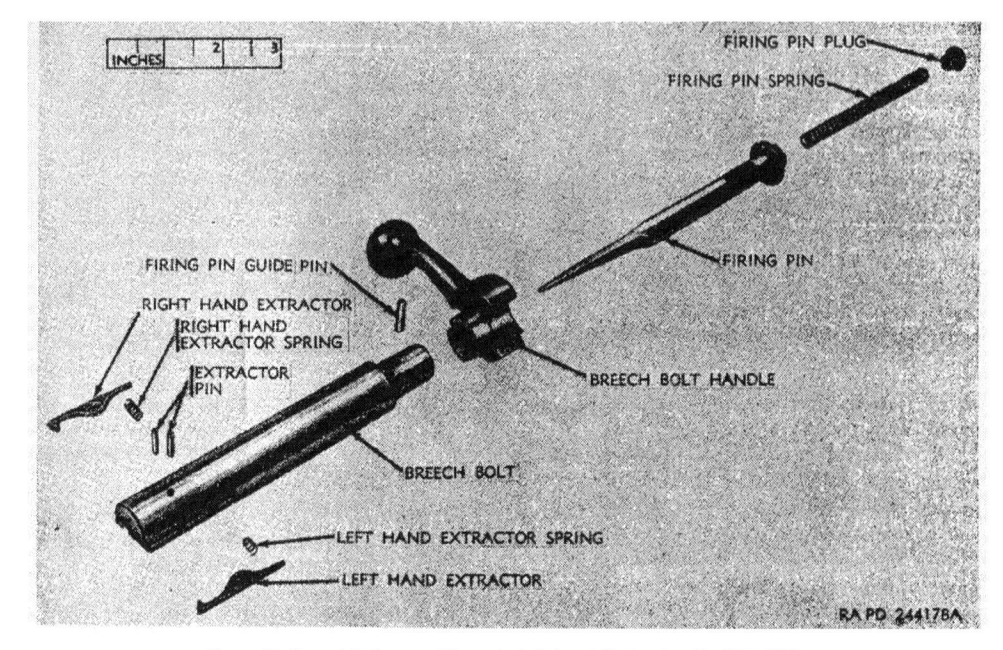

Figure 59. Breech bolt assembly-exploded view (Winchester rifle M52 (HB)).

on the bottom, into its recess in the rear of the breech bolt, and with its firing pin guide pin slot alined with the guide pin hole in the breech bolt shoulder.

(4) Insert a small drift in the rear hole of the firing pin and compress the firing pin spring until the rear end of the spring passes forward of the firing pin guide hole on the breech bolt shoulder. Install firing pin guide pin through the breech bolt and the firing pin. The pin must not protrude from the breech bolt shoulder.

(5) Install the firing pin plug in rear hole of firing pin and tighten.

75. Magazine Assembly.

a. General. The magazine assembly consists of the magazine tube group, the magazine follower, the spring, and base.

b. Maintenance.

(1) Check magazine for fit and retention in the receiver.

(2) Depress the magazine follower and note the smoothness of operation and the tension of the magazine spring.

(3) Check the follower for deformation, wear, and burs, and the spring for set and deformation.

(4) Inspect the magazine for dents, cracks, and deformed lips, and foreign matter.

(5) If any components of the magazine are unserviceable, replace the magazine.

76. Barrel and Receiver Group.

a. General. The barrel will not be disassembled from the receiver. The receiver group consists of the safety lever plate, the breech bolt guide (ejector), the housing assembly, and the magazine and has attached to its exterior the magazine holder assembly and its related parts, the front sight assembly and its dovetail slide, the barrel band, and the two (front and rear) telescope sight mount base assemblies.

b. Disassembly.

Note. The key letters shown below in parentheses refer to figure 60.

AGO 10003A

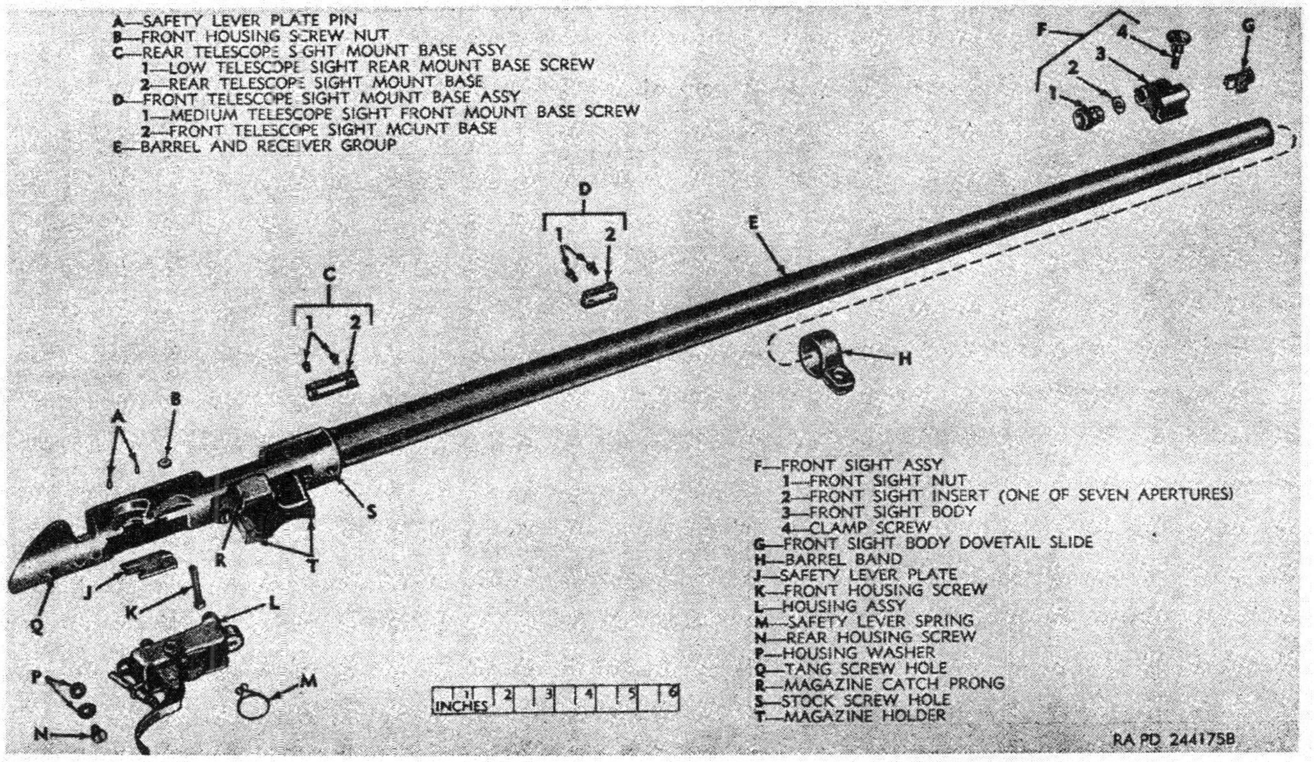
A—SAFETY LEVER PLATE PIN
B—FRONT HOUSING SCREW NUT
C—REAR TELESCOPE SIGHT MOUNT BASE ASSY
1—LOW TELESCOPE SIGHT REAR MOUNT BASE SCREW
2—REAR TELESCOPE SIGHT MOUNT BASE
D—FRONT TELESCOPE SIGHT MOUNT BASE ASSY
1—MEDIUM TELESCOPE SIGHT FRONT MOUNT BASE SCREW
2—FRONT TELESCOPE SIGHT MOUNT BASE
E—BARREL AND RECEIVER GROUP
F—FRONT SIGHT ASSY
1—FRONT SIGHT NUT
2—FRONT SIGHT INSERT (ONE OF SEVEN APERTURES)
3—FRONT SIGHT BODY
4—CLAMP SCREW
G—FRONT SIGHT BODY DOVETAIL SLIDE
H—BARREL BAND
J—SAFETY LEVER PLATE
K—FRONT HOUSING SCREW
L—HOUSING ASSY
M—SAFETY LEVER SPRING
N—REAR HOUSING SCREW
P—HOUSING WASHER
Q—TANG SCREW HOLE
R—MAGAZINE CATCH PRONG
S—STOCK SCREW HOLE
T—MAGAZINE HOLDER
INCHES 1 2 3 4 5 6
RA PD 244175B

Figure 60. Barrel and receiver group with related parts removed (Winchester rifle M52 (HB)).

(1) Unscrew magazine holder front and rear screws from the bottom of the receiver, and remove the magazine holder assembly. Remove breech bolt guide (ejector) from ejection opening of the receiver.

(2) Drift the magazine catch pin out of the side of the holder, and remove magazine catch and spring.

(3) Disengage the rear loop of the safety lever spring (M) from the right end of the safety lever plate activating pin, and loosen the safety lever screw a few turns until the safety lever can be lifted off the right end of the safety lever plate activating pin. Removing the safety lever from the activating pin disconnects the housing assembly from the safety lever plate.

(4) Remove the front housing screw (K) and nut (B) from the receiver.

(5) Remove the rear housing screw (N) and two washers (P) from the receiver.

(6) Disconnect the safety lever plate from the protruding sear pin by pushing the safety lever plate activating pin (fig. 61) forward.

(7) Remove housing assembly (L) from its opening in the receiver and remove the small sear spring.

(8) Unscrew the safety lever screw and nut and remove safety lever (fig. 61) from the center of the housing.

(9) Drift out trigger pin from the bottom of the housing and remove the sear and the trigger (fig. 61) as a unit from the top of the housing. Remove over-travel adjusting screw from the trigger.

(10) Remove the trigger from its aperture in the center of the sear. Remove breech bolt handle plunger locking pin (fig. 61) from the plunger and slide out plunger and plunger spring from the sear.

(11) Slide the trigger pull adjusting spring (fig. 61) from the bottom of the trigger pull adjusting screw and remove screw from housing.

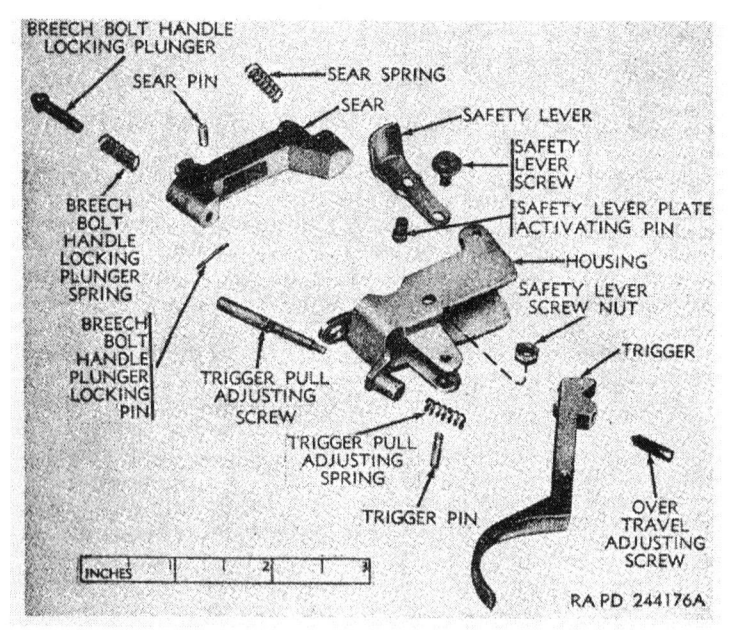

Figure 61. Housing assembly-exploded view (Winchester rifle M52 (HB)).

(12) Disassembly of the Model 52C trigger mechanism will not be attempted.

c. *Maintenance.*
  (1) Inspect all springs for set or kinks and replace if damaged.
  (2) Inspect sear for cracks and wear and replace if damaged.
  (3) Inspect housing for dents and replace if damaged.
  (4) Check magazine lock to determine that it retains magazine properly. Magazine catch shall retain the magazine with sufficient force to prevent removal without releasing the catch.
  (5) Check ejectors for wear on contacting lip.
  (6) See paragraph 57b (2) for barrel inspection instructions.
  (7) Replace worn or broken magazine base and magazine follower.
  (8) Replace defective M52C trigger mechanism.

d. *Assembly.*
  (1) Using the screwdriver 5564038 (fig. 43), screw the trigger pull adjusting screw (fig. 61) into its hole in the front of the housing, and slide its spring over the protruding bottom end of the screw.
  (2) Place sear spring in its seat in the front of the sear (fig. 61). Insert breech bolt handle locking plunger spring in its seat in the front of the sear and insert the locking plunger through the spring; compress the spring and secure in place by installing breech bolt handle plunger locking pin (fig. 61) in hole in bottom of plunger.
  (3) Screw the over-travel adjusting screw (fig. 61) into its hole in the trigger and insert top of trigger through its hole in the sear.
  (4) Install assembled sear and trigger through the top of the housing (fig. 61) and aline trigger pin holes in trigger and housing and insert trigger pin through housing and trigger.
  (5) Aline safety lever (fig. 61) with its hole in the housing, and see that lever thumbpiece is facing up and to the right.
  (6) Install safety lever screw (screw head to the right) through the lever and the housing and secure both of them to the right side of the housing by placing the safety lever screw nut (fig. 61) to the left of the screw and housing wall and by tightening the screw a few turns.
  (7) Slide the safety lever plate (J, fig. 60) in its groove in the receiver to its extreme forward position. Install the housing assembly on the receiver and aline holes; there must be no interference between the safety lever plate and the sear pin.

  Caution: **Do not attempt to force the housing assembly over the safety lever plate, since any force exerted on the plate and pin can damage the thin walled groove in the receiver.**

  Insert the front housing screw from the left side of the receiver and slide the front loop of the safety lever spring over this screw. Install and tighten the front housing screw nut.
  (8) Place rear housing screw and its two washers in housing and tighten screw.
  (9) Place magazine catch spring in its seat in the magazine catch; aline holes in catch and magazine holder, and install magazine catch pin.
  (10) Place magazine holder (magazine opening to the right) on its machined flat surface on the bottom of the receiver, and secure to the receiver with the front magazine holder screws; insert the breech bolt guide (ejector) with its screw hole to the rear and its curved surface to the bottom. Aline the screw holes in the guide with those in the receiver and rear magazine holder screw hole and secure with rear magazine holder screw.
  (11) Insert magazine release plunger with its larger diameter to the left through the opening in the middle of the stock and

AGO 10003A

78

push the plunger all the way to the right Place the barrel and receiver group in groove on top of the stock with holes in the rear and front of the receiver and the hole in the barrel band alined with those in the stock group. Before seating the barrel and receiver group, compress the protruding end of the magazine catch to the left until it is flush with the side of the magazine holder.

Caution: **Do not attempt to force the barrel and receiver group into its seat in the stock, because the sharp bottom end of the magazine catch will damage the wooden stock, when the catch is not completely compressed.**

(12) Insert the tang screw through the rear hole of the receiver and into the stock and tighten the screw.

(13) Insert the barrel band screw through the stock and barrel band and tighten screw.
(14) Insert the stock screw from the bottom of the stock through the front trigger guard hole and stock, and into the threaded hole in the front of the receiver and tighten the screw.
(15) See that the magazine catch has cleared the stock and is located to the left of the magazine release plunger before completely seating the barrel and receiver. Before securing the barrel and receiver group, check for proper assembly by depressing the magazine release plunger on the right side of the stock to see if it moves the magazine catch flush with the right inside wall of the magazine holder. If it does not, remove the barrel and receiver group from the stock group and make another attempt to seat the barrel receiver.

Section VIII. CAL. .22 RIFLE M12 (REMINGTON RIFLE MODEL M40X-S1)

77. Removal and Installation of Subassemblies.

a. See paragraph 49*a* for breakdown of the rifle into the bolt assembly, the receiver sight assembly, the barrel and receiver group, and the stock group.

b. See paragraph 49*b* for installation of subassemblies.

78. Bolt Assembly.

a. General. The bolt assembly consists of the bolt handle body assembly, bolt body, the firing pin and firing spring, the bolt plug, the firing pin head, the right and the left extractor, two extractor plungers, and two extractor springs.

b. Disassembly.

Note. The key letters shown below in parentheses refer to figure 62.

(1) Rotate the safety forward to the FIRE position. Push up on bolt and release in trigger guard, forward of the trigger, and remove bolt assembly (A) from rear of receiver.
(2) Remove two pins from bolt handle body assembly and separate bolt body (A2) from bolt handle body assembly.
(3) Remove firing pin cross pin (A3).

(4) Remove firing spring (A5).
(5) Remove firing pin (A4).
(6) Remove firing pin head (A6).
(7) Unscrew bolt plug (A7).
(8) Remove extractor plunger (A10) and spring (A9) from each side of bolt body and remove extractors (A11).

c. Assembly.

(1) Set firing pin in vise equipped with copper jaws.
(2) Install firing spring over firing pin.
(3) Screw bolt plug into bolt handle body assembly.
(4) Position bolt handle on firing pin and spring, and press down on bolt handle to compress firing spring.
(5) Aline holes in firing pin head and firing pin, and install firing pin cross pin.
(6) Aline bolt body in opening in bolt handle body assembly and install two bolt pins. These pins have a flat side which faces in. One man alines holes on one side of bolt body and bolt handle body assembly while

AGO 10003A

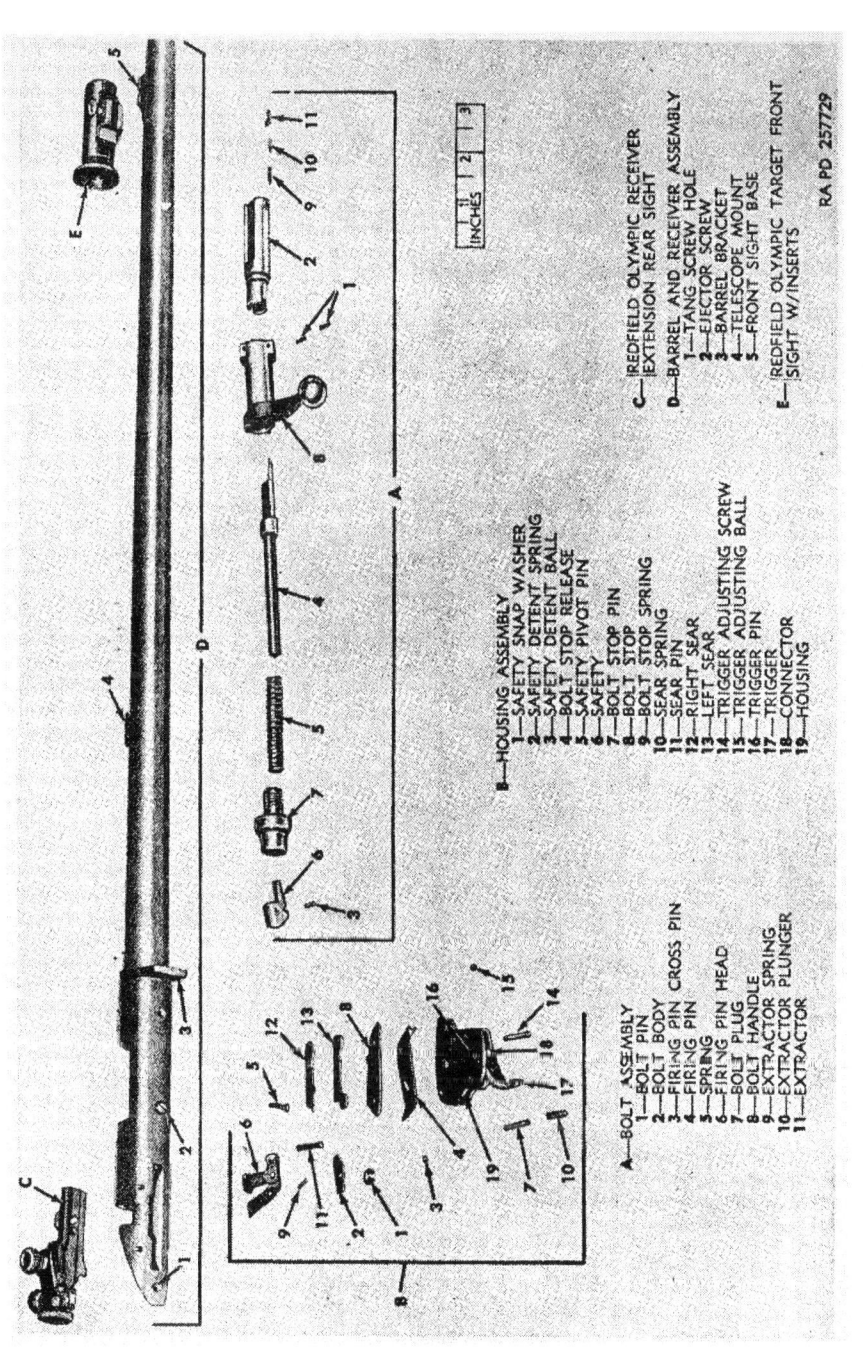

Figure 62. Barrel, receiver, and bolt group-exploded view (Remington rifle M40X-S1).

the other drives in opposite pin.

79. Trigger Housing Assembly.
Note. The key letters shown below in parentheses refer to figure 62.

a. Removal. Remove two pins securing trigger housing assembly to receiver and remove housing assembly (B).

b. Disassembly.
(1) Remove safety snap washer (B1).
(2) Remove safety detent spring (B2).
(3) Remove safety detent ball (B3).
(4) Remove bolt stop release (B4).
(5) Remove safety pivot pin (B5).
(6) Remove safety (B6).
(7) Remove bolt stop pin (B7).
(8) Remove bolt stop (B8).
(9) Remove bolt stop spring (B9).
(10) Remove sear spring (B10).
(11) Remove sear pin (short) (B11).
(12) Remove left sear (B13).
(13) Remove right sear (B12).
(14) Remove trigger adjusting screw (B14).
(15) Remove trigger adjusting ball (B15).
(16) Remove trigger spring.
(17) Remove trigger pin from housing (B19) and remove trigger stop screw, trigger, and connector only if replacement is required.

c. Assembly.
(1) Position trigger and connector in housing and install trigger pivot pin. Position trigger housing in opening in receiver and from top of receiver install right and left sear. Left sear has a ball notch. Secure with sear pin (short).
(2) Install trigger adjusting spring and ball, and trigger adjusting screw and stop screw.
(3) Position sear spring on inside of trigger housing and compress both sears and install bolt stop pin (long) over sears.
(4) Position bolt stop spring in groove in receiver and install bolt stop on free end of bolt stop pin and secure trigger housing to receiver with this pin.

(5) Install bolt stop release.
(6) Install safety.
(7) Install safety pivot pin.
(8) Install safety detent ball and spring.
(9) Install safety snap washer facing the bolt.

80. Stock Group.
a. Disassembly.
(1) Remove butt pad screws.
(2) Remove pad.
(3) Remove front, center, and rear guard screws (fig. 50) that hold trigger guard to receiver and stock.
(4) Remove trigger guard (fig. 50) and guide plate.
(5) Remove front swivel screw and remove front swivel block and front swivel nut.
(6) Remove front swivel, base screws, and base (fig. 63).
(7) Remove barrel bedding screws (fig. 63) and spring.

b. Maintenance.
(1) Inspect the stock for cracks, gouges, or dents. Remove any roughness or splinters from wood with fine grade sandpaper. Preserve stocks as described in paragraph 36.
(2) Check the butt plate for proper sealing. Make certain that there are no loose or missing screws.
(3) Examine forearm swivels for secure mounting.

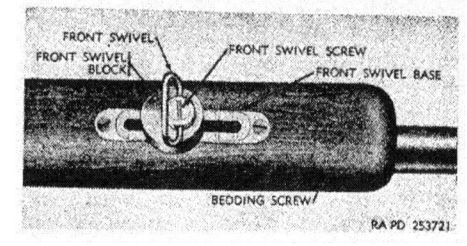

Figure 63. Front swivel assembly (Remington

AGO 10003A

(4) Inspect trigger guard and trigger guard plate for loose screws, burs, or damaged parts.
c. *Assembly.*
(1) Install stock on barrel and receiver.
(2) Install trigger guide plate over trigger housing.
(3) Install trigger guard and secure with front center and rear guard screws (fig. 50).

Section IX. CAL..30-06 WINCHESTER RIFLE MODEL 70 (SPECIAL MATCH GRADE)

81. Removal and Installation of Subassemblies.

a. See paragraph 50a for breakdown of the weapon into the stock assembly, barrel and receiver group, bolt assembly, Lyman rear sight No. 48WH, and Lyman front sight No. 77.

b. See paragraph 50b for installation of subassemblies.

82. Stock Assembly.

a. General. No disassembly of the stock assembly is authorized.

b. Maintenance.
(1) Examine butt plate for looseness on stock. Examine forearm swivels for secure mounting.
(2) Remove any roughness or splinters from wood with fine grade sandpaper. Preserve stock as described in paragraph 36.

83. Bolt Assembly.

a. General. The bolt assembly consists mainly of the bolt sleeve assembly, firing pin group, and extractor group.

b. Disassembly.
(1) Depress the bolt sleeve lock.
(2) Turn the breech bolt sleeve assembly counterclockwise and remove the firing pin and sleeve (fig. 64) from the bolt.
(3) Put safety lock in FIRE position (par. 15e).
(4) Depress firing pin sleeve slightly and turn firing pin to aline rectangular slot of the sleeve with the firing pin. Remove sleeve and firing pin spring from pin.
(5) Unscrew firing pin stop screw from sleeve and withdraw sleeve from the firing pin body.
(6) Slide extractor clockwise on bolt to remove extractor from bolt lug. Slide the extractor forward to remove extractor from extractor ring. Remove ring (fig. 65) from bolt.

c. *Maintenance.*
(1) Inspect the firing pin for worn or mushroomed end; replace if necessary. Check firing pin spring for kinks or set; replace if necessary.
(2) Inspect the extractor for bending, burs, or excessive wear in the extractor ring grooves; replace if necessary. Replace bent or broken extractor rings.
(3) Inspect breech bolt sleeve assembly for a worn safety lock, sleeve lock spring, or firing pin stop screw. Replace sleeve assembly, if necessary.

d. Assembly.
(1) Insert the extractor ring onto groove in bolt. Slide the extractor slot onto lips of extractor. Rotate the extractor counterclockwise on the bolt until end of extractor seats onto lug in front of the bolt.
(2) Insert breech bolt sleeve assembly on firing pin and screw on the firing pin stop screw.
(3) Install firing pin spring and firing pin sleeve on the firing pin. Aline rectangular slot in sleeve with firing pin and depress the spring. Rotate sleeve to hold the spring depressed.
(4) Put the safety lock in FIRE position (par. 15e).
(5) Screw the breech bolt sleeve assembly onto the bolt until it is held in place by the bolt sleeve lock.

84. Lyman Front Sight No. 77.

a. Disassembly. Disassemble Lyman front sight No. 77 as described in paragraph 17.

AGO 10000A

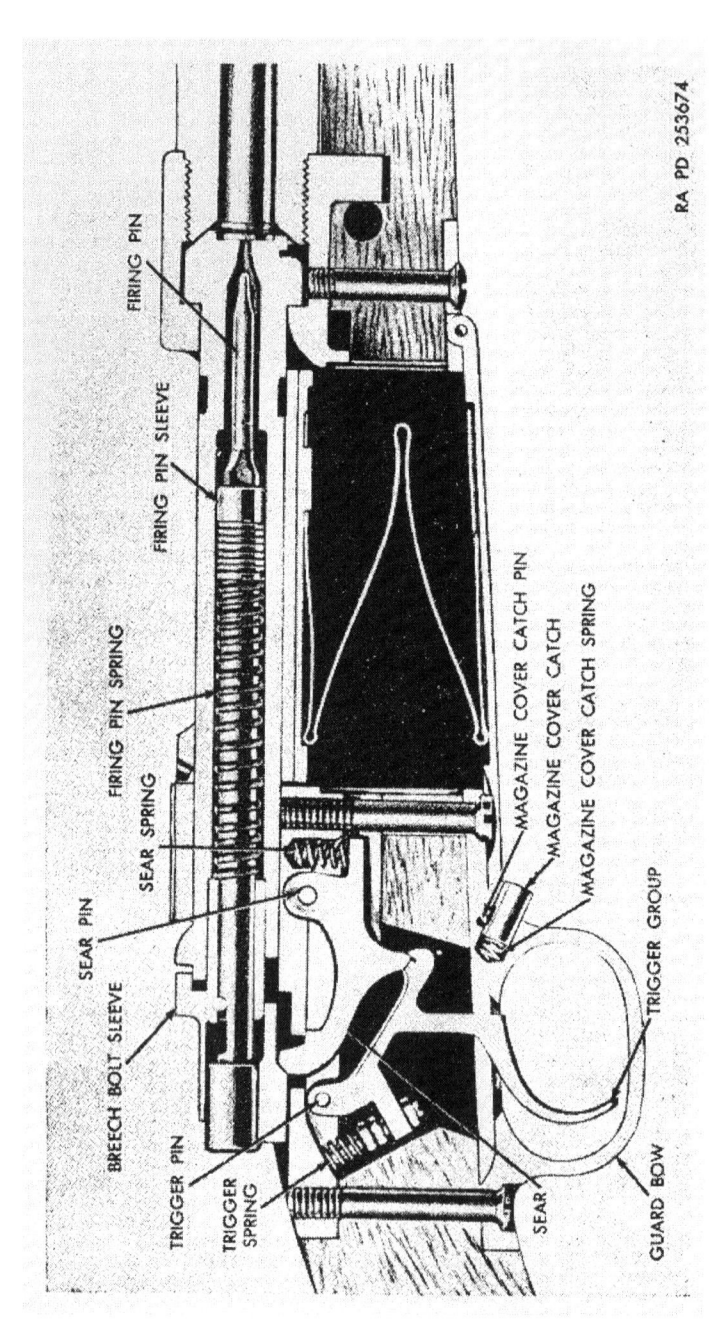

Figure 64. Cal. .30-06 Winchester rifle model 70 (special match grade)-cross section.

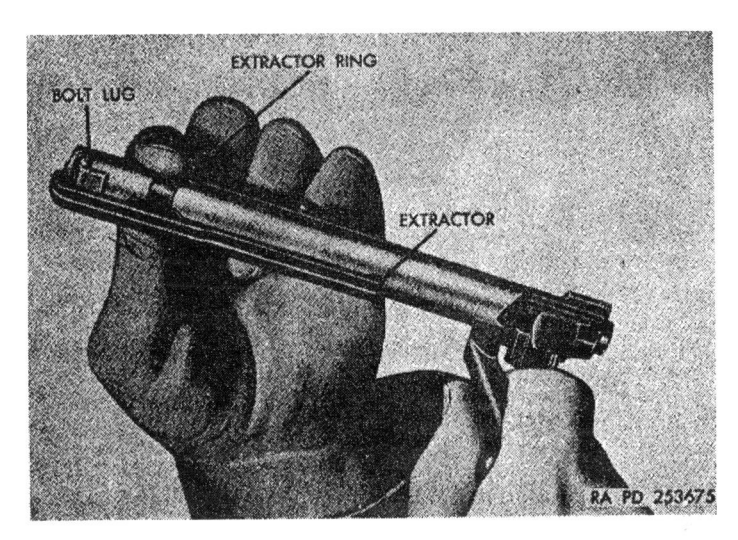

Figure 65. Bolt assembly (Winchester rifle model 70).

   b. Maintenance.
     (1) Replace inserts if they are worn or broken.
     (2) Replace worn or broken insert holding nut and base locking bolt.
   c. Assembly. Assemble the Lyman front sight No. 77 as described in paragraph 17.

85. Lyman Rear Sight 48WH.

   a. Removal. Unscrew the rear sight lock bolt knob as far as possible, press it in, and at the same time, lift the rear sight slide up sufficiently to expose the short rear sight mounting screw underneath the left side of the slide. Remove the short rear sight mounting screw. Remove the other mounting screw and rear sight slide.
   b. Disassembly (fig. 66).
     (1) With a small jeweler's screwdriver, loosen the windage screw knob setscrew in the windage screw knob, and remove the knob and rear sight click spring. Remove the two windage cap screws from the windage cap and remove the cap.
     (2) Unscrew the rear sight aperture disk from the rear sight aperture.
     (3) Remove the rear sight aperture and rear sight windage screw. Remove the screw from the aperture.
     (4) Unscrew the two rear sight windage scale screws and remove the rear sight windage scale.
     (5) With a split-type screwdriver, remove the elevating screw nut on the bottom of the elevating screw and remove the elevating screw, elevating screw knob, and washer. The knob may be removed from the screw by loosening the elevating screw knob setscrew in the knurled portion with a jeweler's screwdriver.
     (6) Remove the rear sight lock bolt knob setscrew from the center of the lock bolt knob, and remove the rear sight lock bolt knob and lock bolt spring. Remove the lock bolt.
     (7) Remove the rear sight pointer screw and rear sight pointer.
     (8) The rear sight stop screw can be removed by unscrewing it from the slide.
   c. Maintenance.
     (1) Check that sight slide is free to move in sight base.
     (2) Check the functioning of the click springs under the elevation screw knob or windage screw knob.
     (3) Check the aperture disk for looseness or burs.

AGO 10003A

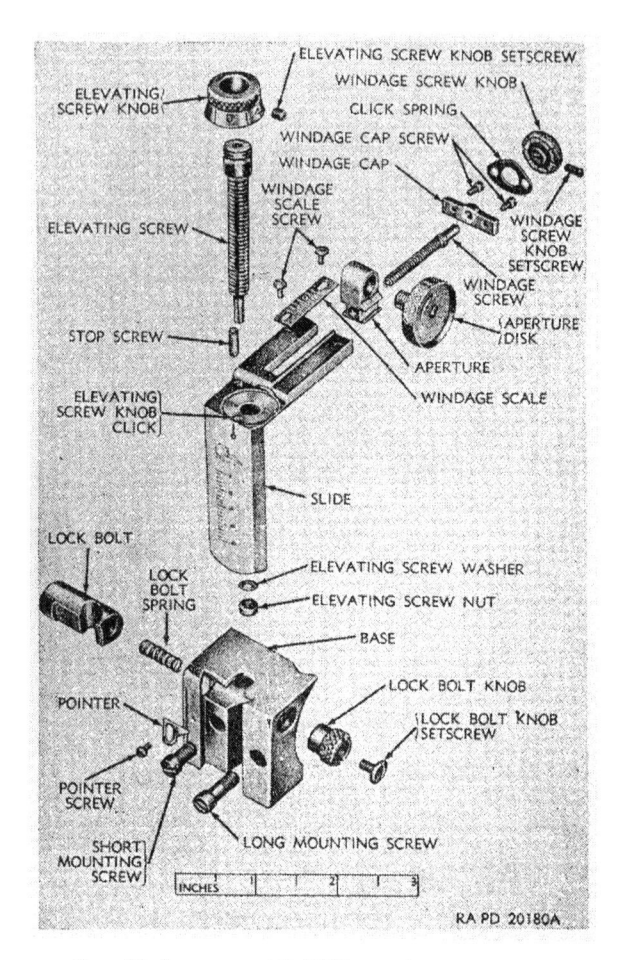

Figure 66. Lyman rear sight 48WH assembly-exploded view.

(4) Check functioning of the lock bolt knob.
(5) Check "numbers" on windage scale and sight slide for wear.
(6) Examine threads of elevation screw and windage screw for wear or burs.

d. *Assembly* (fig. 66).
(1) Insert the rear sight lock bolt and lock bolt spring into the rear sight base.

(2) Place the lock bolt knob on the lock bolt and install the lock bolt knob set screw in the center of the knob.
(3) Assemble the rear sight elevating screw knob on the elevating screw and tighten the elevating screw knob set screw in the knob. Install the rear sight stop screw in the rear sight slide and adjust it for zero elevation. Install the elevating screw in

the slide, and install the elevating screw knob click spring and click. Push the elevating screw into place, press the elevating screw knob against the slide, and install the elevating screw washer and slotted elevating screw nut on the end of the elevating screw. Tighten the nut with a split screwdriver.

(4) Position the rear sight windage scale and secure it with two windage scale screws.

(5) Slide the rear sight aperture into the windage slide with the beveled lip extending over the windage scale. Assemble the rear sight windage screw into the rear sight aperture. Install the windage cap and secure it in place with the two windage cap screws. Install the rear sight click spring and secure the windage screw knob against it by tightening the windage screw knob set screw in the knob.

(6) Screw the rear sight aperture disk into the rear sight aperture.

(7) Unscrew the rear sight lock bolt knob as far as possible. Press in on the knob and insert the elevating slide into the rear sight base.

(8) Install the pointer and secure with pointer screw.

e. Installation. Place the rear sight base in position on the receiver with the rear sight slide removed to expose the hole for the short rear sight mounting screw. Install the short and long rear sight mounting screws. Press in on the rear sight lock bolt and push the rear sight slide down into position.

86. Receiver Group

a. General. The barrel will not be disassembled from the receiver. The receiver group consists mainly of the trigger group, bolt stop group, sear group, and magazine group. The magazine group was disassembled on field stripping the rifle.

b. Disassembly.

(1) Drive out the trigger pin. Remove the trigger assembly and trigger spring.

(2) Remove the bolt stop, bolt stop plunger, and plunger spring.

(3) Drive out the sear pin and remove the sear and sear spring.

c. Maintenance.

(1) Inspect the trigger spring for set or kink; replace if necessary.

(2) Check bolt stop plunger for wear; replace if broken. Check tension in bolt stop spring; replace if set or broken.

(3) Inspect sear for worn surfaces; replace if necessary.

(4) See paragraph 60b(2) for barrel inspection instructions.

(5) Replace worn or broken magazine, magazine cover, and magazine follower.

d. Assembly.

(1) Insert sear spring into well and install sear into the slot in the receiver; then drive in the sear pin.

(2) Insert the bolt stop plunger spring and plunger into well in left side of receiver. Install the bolt stop into slot in receiver.

(3) Insert the trigger spring into the well in the receiver. Insert the trigger assembly over the spring and drive in the trigger pin.

(4) Test the trigger pull using weights. The trigger should release sear with a 5-pound weight and should not release it with a 4 1/2-pound weight.

87. Guard Bow Group

a. General. The guard bow group consists of the magazine cover catch, magazine cover catch spring, and guard bow.

b. Disassembly. Drive out the cover catch pin, and remove the magazine cover catch and cover catch spring from the guard bow.

c. Maintenance. Replace a broken or set cover catch spring. Stone the magazine cover catch with a fine stone to remove any burs.

d. Assembly. Insert the magazine cover catch and cover catch spring into the well in the guard bow. Depress the catch, aligning the groove on the catch with the hole in the bow, and drive in the cover catch spring.

Section X. SIGHTS

88. Receiver Extension Rear Sight Assembly-Lyman Rear Sight No. 525

a. General. The receiver extension rear sight assembly consists of the rear sight base, with its filler and binding screws; the rear sight receiver base; the elevation take-up plug; the rear sight elevation screw; elevation knob; click elevation spring; set screws and adjusting screws; graduated elevation plate and screw; the rear sight windage screw; windage cap and screws; windage knob and set screw; click windage spring; graduated windage scale and screw; and the rear sight slide, aperture, and disk.

b. Maintenance.
(1) Try the rear sight elevation and windage knobs for tension.
(2) Check the aperture for burs or looseness.
(3) See that the elevation and windage scales are clear and readable.
(4) Check for damaged or loose components and replace damaged items.

c. Disassembly.
(1) Remove the two receiver base mounting screws and remove receiver extension rear sight.
(2) Remove rear sight-base binding screw and filler screw (fig. 67) and separate rear sight base from rear sight receiver base.
(3) Remove two windage cap screws (fig. 67) and withdraw windage cap, rear sight aperture, and attached parts from rear slide.
　(a) Remove rear sight disk from aperture (fig. 67).
　(b) Remove rear sight windage screw (fig. 67) from aperture and windage cap.
　(c) Remove windage knob setscrew (fig. 67) and separate knob and click windage spring from rear sight windage screw.
　(d) Remove windage scale screw and remove graduated windage scale (fig. 67).
(4) Remove elevation plate screw (fig. 67) and remove graduated elevation plate.
(5) Remove rear sight elevation screw (fig. 67) from rear sight slide and base and separate slide from base.
　(a) Remove elevation knob adjusting screw (fig. 67) from end of elevation screw.
　(b) Remove two set screws from elevation knob and remove knob.
　(c) Remove click elevation spring from recess in slide.
　(d) Remove elevation take-up plug from base.

d. Maintenance.
(1) Check slide for freedom of movement in base.
(2) Check click springs for proper functioning and tension.
(3) Check aperture disk for looseness or burs.
(4) Check graduated plates, scales, and knobs for clearness of graduations.
(5) Examine threads of elevation screw and windage screw for crossing, deformation, and burs.

e. Assembly.
(1) Install the rear right slide (fig. 67) in the rear sight base (fig. 67) and install rear sight elevation screw through slide and base.
(2) Install click elevation spring in recess on top of rear sight elevation screw and position in place.
(3) Install elevation knob on end of rear sight elevation screw (fig. 67) align 0 graduation marks on knob and slide. Install two set screws in knob. Install elevation knob adjusting screw (fig, 67) in top of knob.
(4) Install rear sight aperture in groove of rear right slide.
(5) Install rear sight disk in rear sight aperture.
(6) Position windage cap (fig. 67) on end of groove in rear sight slide and secure with two windage cap screws.
(7) Install rear sight windage screw (fig. 67) through holes in windage cap and rear

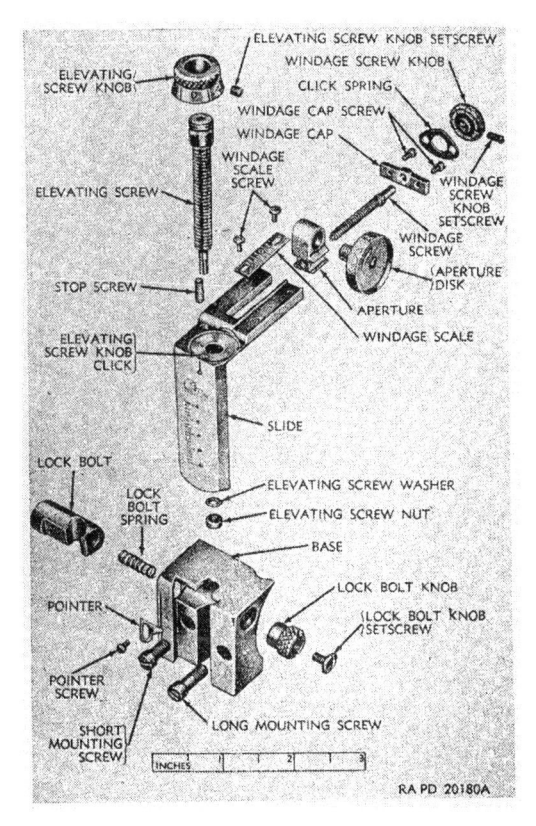

Figure 67. Receiver extension rear sight assembly-exploded view (Lyman rear sight No. 525)

sight aperture and seat shoulder on threaded end in hole in sleeve.

(8) Install click windage spring and windage knob (fig. 67) over end of rear sight windage screw and secure with windage knob set screw.

(9) Install graduated windage scale (fig. 67) and secure with windage scale screw. Align reference marks on rear sight aperture and windage scale.

(10) Install graduated elevation plate (fig. 67) on rear sight slide and secure with elevation plate screw.

(11) Secure rear sight receiver base to receiver with concave surface in contact with receiver and secure with two receiver base mounting screws.

(12) Install elevation take-up plug.

(13) Secure rear sight base to rear sight receiver base and secure with rear sight base binding screw and fill screw

t. Installation. Install the receiver extension rear right assembly on mount on the left-rear side of the receiver, with the concave side of the rear sight receiver base to the right and the rear sight disk to the rear. Align holes in receiver base with those in the receiver mount and secure with two receiver base mounting screws.

89. Redfield Olympic Target Front Sight Assembly

a. The top of the barrel near the muzzle is drilled and tapped to receive the front sight base with its two mounting screws.

b. The front sight assembly slides over this dovetail-shaped base from the rear and is secured to the base by the front sight screw.

c. Plastic inserts are furnished for use in the front sight. To install insert, unscrew funnel-shaped end of sight and drop insert in position in slot. Tighten funnel-shaped end.

Section XI. FINAL INSPECTION

90. General

The acceptance standard of a weapon for service, which has undergone repairs, is its ability to perform its cyclic operation with a smooth mechanical action. It will be necessary, therefore, for the responsible maintenance or manufacturer's personnel to test the weapon by function firing and zeroing.

91. Final Inspection Procedures

a. Check usual appearance of weapon.

b. Check the operation and functioning of the weapon.

c. Examine weapon for proper lubrication or preservative (par. 36).

d. Function fire the weapon.

e. Inspect and zero the weapon (par. 57)

CHAPTER 5
AMMUNITION

92. General

The cartridge, as issued, is a complete assembly consisting of all the components necessary to fire the weapon once. These components are the bullet, cartridge case, propellant, and primer. For complete information on classification, care, handling, preservation, packing, marking, and component parts of small-arms ammunition, see TM 9-1990. For information concerning misfires and hangfires, and for precautions in firing small-arms cartridges, see paragraph 36, TM 9-1990 and AR 385-63.

93. Identification

Small-arms cartridges used in the weapons covered in this technical manual are identified by the markings on the packing boxes, the cartons, and on the cartridge case heads. For complete information on identification of small arms cartridges, see TM 9-1990.

94. Authorized Cartridges

The cartridges authorized for use in the weapons covered in this technical manual are listed in table V. The nomenclature used in the table completely identifies each item except for ammunition lot number.

Table V. Authorized Cartridges

Weapon in which used	Cartridge
Cal..22	
Pistol, automatic, cal..22 Ruger Mark I (target model) (6%7 in. bbl) or Pistol, automatic, cal..22 high standard (supermatic) and Rifle, cal..22, M12 (Winchester model 52 or Remington model 40X-S1).	CARTRIDGE, CAL..22: ball, long rifle (40 grain) Western Super Match Mk II or equivalent Xpert or equivalent.
Cal 30-06	
Rifle, cal 30-06, Winchester, model &0 (special match grade).	CARTRIDGE, CAL 30-06: ball, 180 grain 1 Remington Palmer Match or equivalent Remington Palmer Match or equivalent 2 Western Super Match (hand loaded) or equivalent
Cal 38 Special	
Revolver, Smith and Wesson, cal 38 special, K-38 (masterpiece).	CARTRIDGE, CAL 38 SPECIAL: ball, mid-range, 146 grain bullet (wad cutter). Western Super Match or equivalent

1 The bullets have metal jackets and tapered bases.
2 Bullet seated to depth suitable for magazine loading.

CHAPTER 6
SHIPMENT AND STORAGE

95. Shipping Instructions

a. Responsibility. When shipping small arms weapons, the unit commander will be responsible for shipping the materiel adequately processed, packaged, and packed as prescribed in c below.

b. Army Shipping Documents. Prepare all Army shipping documents accompanying freight in accordance with AR 725-5.

c. Preparation for Shipment.

(1) Materiel removed from storage for shipment must not be reprocessed, unless inspection reveals it to be inadequately processed, packaged, and packed for shipment.

(2) Preservation, packaging, and packing must be sufficient to protect the materiel against deterioration and damage during shipment (TB ORD 623 and TM 9-1005). Under no condition will the materiel with critical surfaces be packaged without benefit of sufficient preservatives to insure adequate protection of materiel. Materiel will be marked in accordance with TM 9-1005.

96. Limited Storage Instructions

a. Materiel will be processed, packaged, and packed for limited storage as prescribed in paragraph 95c(2).

b. Storage of materiel will be in accordance with TM 743-200-1 and SB 38-8-1.

APPENDIX
REFERENCES

1. Publication Indexes
The following indexes should be consulted frequently for latest changes or revisions of references given in this appendix and for new publications relating to materiel covered in this manual.

Index of Army Motion Pictures, Film Strips, Slides and Phono-Recordings	DA Pam 108-1
Military Publications:	
Index of Administrative Publications	DA Pam 310-1
Index of Blank Forms	DA Pam 310-2
Index of Graphic Training Aids and Devices	DA Pam 310-5
Index of Supply Manuals Ordnance Corps	DA Pam 310-29
Index of Technical Manuals, Technical Bulletins, Supply Bulletins, Lubrication Orders, and Modification Work Orders.	DA Pam 310-4
Index of Training Publications	DA Pam 310-3

2. Supply Manuals
The following manuals of the Department of the Army supply manual pertain to this materiel:

a. Ammunition.

Ammunition, through 30 millimeter	SM 9-5-1305

b. General.

Introduction	ORD 1

c. Repair and Rebuild.

Army Rifle and Pistol Teams (Regular Army, Reserve Components and ROTC).	TA 60-18
Shop Set, Small Arms, Field Maintenance	SM 9-4-5180-J-6
Special Tool Sets for Small Arms and Automatic Weapons	ORD 6 SNL J-12
Tool Kit, Small Arms Repairman (MOS 421.10)	SM 9-4-5180-J10-2
Weapons (Class 1005 Guns through 30-mm); (Class 1010 Guns over 30-mm up to 75-mm); (Class 1015 Guns 75-mm through 125-mm).	SM 9-5-1000

d. Weapons.

Pistol, Automatic, Cal22, High Standard, Supermatic; Pistol, Automatic, Cal22, Ruger. Mark I, Target Model.	ORD 7 SNL B-49
Revolver, Colt, Cal38, Special, Detective Special, 2-Inch Barrel; Revolver, Colt, Cal38, Special, Official Police, 2- and 4-Inch Barrel; Revolver, Smith and Wesson, Cal38, Military and Police, 4-Inch Barrel; Revolver, Smith and Wesson, Cal38, Special, K38 Masterpiece; Revolver, Smith and Wesson, Cal38, Special Military and Police, 2- and 4-Inch Barrel.	ORD 7 SNL B-29
Rifle, Cal22, Stevens, Model 416-2, Target; Rifle, Cal22, Remington, Model 513T, Matchmaster; Rifle, Cal22, Winchester, Model 52, Heavy Barrel; Rifle, Cal22, Winchester, Model 75, Target.	ORD 7 SNL B-25
Rifle, Cal30-06, Winchester, Model 70, Special Match Grade; Rifle, Cal. .300H and H Magnum, Winchester, Model 70, Bull Gun.	ORD 7 SNL B-50

3. Forms

The following forms pertain to this materiel:
DA Form 5-31, Shop Job Order Register
DA Form 9-79, Parts Requisition
DA Form 9-80, Job Order File
DA Form 9-81, Exchange Part of Unit Identification Tag
DA Form 421, Stock Record Card
DA Form 828, Job Time Ticket-Individual
DA Form 829, Rejection Memorandum
DA Form 1546, Request for Issue or Turn-In
DA Form 2028, Recommended Changes to DA Technical Manual Parts List or Supply Manual 7, 8, or 9.
DD Form 6, Report of Damaged or Improper Shipment

4. Other Publications

The following explanatory publications contain information pertinent to this materiel and associated equipment:

a. Ammunition.

Ammunition, General	TM 9-1900
	TOA IIA-1-20
Ammunition Inspection Guide	TM 9-1904
Ballistic Data, Performance of Ammunition	TM 9-1907
Disposal of Supplies and Equipment: Ammunition	AR 755-140-1
Qualification in Arms: Qualification and Familiarization	AR 370-5
Safety: Regulations for Firing Ammunition for Training, Target Practice, and Combat.	AR 385-63
	AFR 50-13
Small-Arms Ammunition	TM 9-1990
Training Ammunition	TA 23-100

b. General.

Instruction Guide: Operation and Maintenance of Ordnance Materiel in Extreme Cold (0° to -65° F.).	TM 9-2855
Logistics (General): Malfunctions Involving Ammunition and Explosives	AR 700-1300-8
Military Symbols	FM 21-30
	AFM 55-3
Military Terms, Abbreviations, and Symbols:	
Authorized Abbreviations	AR 320-50
Dictionary of United States Army Terms	AR 320-5
Military Training	FM 21-5
Ordnance Maintenance and General Supply in the Field	FM 9-10
Safety:	
Accident Reporting and Records	AR 385-40
Regulations for Firing Ammunition for Training, Target Practice, and Combat.	AR 385-63
Stock Control: Common Classification Code	AR 711-50
Supplies and Equipment: Unsatisfactory Equipment Report	AR 700-38
Techniques of Military Instruction	FM 21-6

c. Repair and Rebuild.

Cleaning and Black Finishing of Ferrous Metals	TM 9-1861
Commercial revolvers: Repair and Replacement Parts	SB 9-135
Lubrication	TM 9-2833

AGO 10003A

Maintenance and Care of Hand Tools	TM 9-867
Maintenance of Supplies and Equipment: Maintenance Responsibilities and Shop Operation.	AR 750-5
Operation and Maintenance: Cal..22 High Standard Automatic Pistol (Supermatic), Cal..22 Ruger Mark I Automatic Pistol (Target Model), Cal 38 Special Revolver K-38 (Masterpiece), and Cal 30-06 Winchester Rifle Model 70.	TM 9-2316
Ordnance Maintenance: Materials Used For Cleaning, Preserving, Abrasing, and Cementing Ordnance Materiel and Related Materials Including Chemicals, Lubricants, Indicators, and Hydraulic Fluids.	TM 9-1007
Repair and Replacement of Parts for Commercial Pistols	SB 9-125
Repair and Replacement Parts for Commercial Revolvers	SB 9-112
Small Arms Accidents, Malfunctions, and Their Causes	TM 9-2210

d. Shipment and Storage.

Preparation Processing and Documentation for Requisitioning, Shipping and Receiving.	AR 725-5
Instruction Guide: Ordnance Preservation, Packaging, Packing, Storage and Shipping.	TM 9-1005
Logistics (General): Report of Damaged or Improper Shipment	AR 700-58
Ordnance Operational List of Specifications and Instructions for Packaging and Processing General Supplies.	SB 9-156
Methods of Preservation	MILP-116
Packaging and Shipping of Materiel:	
Preparation of Freight for Air Shipments	TB 38-230-1
Preservation, Packaging, and Packing of Military Supplies and Equipment.	TM 38-230
Packaging of Small Arms Materiel with Volatile Corrosion Inhibitor (VCI).	TB ORD 623
Protection of Ordnance General Supplies in Open Storage	TB ORD 379
Storage and Materials Handling	TM 743-200-1
Storage and Shipment of Supplies and Equipment: Preservation, Packaging, and Packing.	AR 740-15
Storage of Army Supplies and Equipment in Shed and Open Storage	SB 38-8-1
Storage of Supplies and Equipment: Shed and Open Storage Supplies	AR 743-41

AGO 10003A

INDEX

	Paragraph	Page
Accidents, field report	2e	3
Ammunition:		
Authorized cartridges	94	90
General	92	90
Identification	93	90
Assembly (See specific items)		
Authorized forms	2b	3
Barrel and receiver group:		
Cal..22 rifle M12 (Winchester rifle, Model 52) (heavy barrel):		
Assembly	76d	78
Description	76a	75
Disassembly	76b	75
Maintenance	76c	78
Cal..22 Ruger Mark I automatic pistol (target model):		
Assembly	65e	68
Disassembly	65a	68
Maintenance	65b	68
Barrel assembly (cal..22 high-standard automatic pistol (supermatic)):		
Assembly	60c	63
Disassembly	60a	62
Maintenance	60b	62
Bolt assembly:		
Cal..22 rifle M12 (Remington rifle Model 40X-S1):		
Assembly	78c	79
Description	78a	79
Disassembly	78b	79
Cal..22 Ruger Mark I automatic pistol (target model):		
Assembly	67d	69
Description	67a	68
Disassembly	67b	68
Maintenance	67e	68
Cal 30-06 Winchester rifle Model 70 (special match grade):		
Assembly	83d	82
Description	83a	82
Disassembly	83b	82
Maintenance	83c	82
Breech bolt assembly (cal..22 rifle M12 (Winchester rifle, Model 52 (heavy barrel)):		
Assembly	74d	74
Description	74a	74
Disassembly	74b	74
Maintenance e	74e	74

	Paragraph	Page
Cal..22 High-Standard automatic pistol (supermatic):		
Cleaning (after firing)	38d(3)	46
Description	3a	4
Field stripping	45	51
Firing (operation under usual conditions)	20b	34
Inspection	57a	59
Loading (operation under usual conditions)	20a	33
Lubrication	36b	44
Name and data plates	4a	12
Subassemblies:		
Installation	45b	51
Removal	45a	51
Tabulated data	5a	15
Unloading (operation under usual conditions)	20c	34
Cal..22 Rifle M12 (Remington Model 40X-SI):		
Cleaning (after firing S	38d(1)	45
Description	3d(2)	12
Field stripping	49	55
Firing (under usual conditions)	24b	37
Inspection	57d(2)	61
Loading (under usual conditions)	24a	37
Lubrication	36e	44
Name and data plates	4e	15
Subassemblies:		
Installation	49b	55
Removal	49a	55
Tabulated data	5e	15
Cal..22 Rifle M12 (Winchester Model 52, Heavy Barrel):		
Cleaning (after firing)	38d(1)	45
Description	3d	4
Field stripping	48	53
Firing (under usual conditions)	23b	37
Inspection	57d(1)	60
Loading (under usual conditions)	23a	36
Lubrication	36e	44
Name and data plates	4d	15
Subassemblies:		
Installation	48b	55
Removal	48a	53
Tabulated data	5d	15)
Unloading (under usual conditions)	23c	37
Cal..22 Ruger Mark I automatic pistol (target model) (67⅞-in. barrel):		
Cleaning (after firing)	38d(3)	46
Description	3b	4

AGO 10003A

	Paragraph	Page
Cal..22 Ruger Mark I automatic pistol (target model) (6⅞7-in. barrel)-Continued		
Field stripping	46	52
Inspection	57b	60
Loading (under usual conditions)	21a	34
Lubrication	36c	44
Name and data plates	4b	12
Subassemblies:		
Installation	46b	52
Removal	46a	52
Tabulated data	5b	15
Unloading (under usual conditions)	21c	35
Cal 38 Special, Smith and Wesson revolver K-38 (masterpiece):		
Assembly	72	73
Cleaning (after firing)	38d(2)	46
Description	3c	4
Disassembly	70	71
Field stripping	47	53
Firing (under usual conditions)	22b	36
Inspection	57c,71	60,73
Loading (under usual conditions)	22a	35
Lubrication	36d	44
Maintenance	71	73
Name and data plates	4c	12
Subassemblies:		
Installation	47b	53
Removal	47a	53
Tabulated data	5c	15
Unloading (under usual conditions)	22c	36
Cal 30-06 Winchester rifle Model 70 (Special Match Grade)		
Cleaning (after firing)	38d(1)	45
Description	3e	12
Field stripping	50	57
Firing (under usual conditions)	25b	38
Inspection	57e	61
Loading (under usual conditions)	25a	37
Lubrication	36e	44
Name and data plates	4f	15
Subassemblies:		
Installation	46b	52
Removal	46a	52
Tabulated data	5f	16
Unloading (under usual conditions)	25c	38
Cleaning:		
After firing	38d	45
Before firing	38c	45
Daily	38b	45
General	38a	45
Service periods up to 1 week	38e	46
(See also specific items)		
Cold-weather conditions	28	39
Controls and instruments:		
Cal..22 High-Standard automatic pistol (supermatic):		
Adjustable rear sight assembly	10g	20
Barrel plunger	10f	20
Barrel weights		10d18

	Paragraph	Page
Controls and instruments-Continued		
Cal..22 High-Standard automatic pistol (supermatic)-Continued		
Magazine assembly	10	18
Magazine catch	10a	18
Rear sight elevation screw	10g (2)	20
Rear sight windage screw	10g (3)	20
Safety lever	10b	18
Slide assembly	10h	20
Slide lock lever	10e	20
Cal..22 Rifle M12 receiver extension rear sight assembly:		
Description	18a	81
Knobs, scales, and disk	18b	82
Removal and installation	18c	83
Cal..22 Rifle M12 (Remington Model 40X-S1):		
Bolt assembly	14b	26
Bolt handle	14a	26
Magazine	14c	26
Safety	14d	26
Trigger	14e	26
Cal..22 Rifle M12 (Winchester rifle Model 52, heavy barrel):		
Breech bolt handle	13a	26
Magazine	13b	26
Safety lever	13c	26
Cal..22 Ruger Mark I automatic pistol (target model) (6⅞7-in. barrel):		
Bolt assembly	11c	20
Magazine assembly	11e	24
Magazine catch	11b	20
Micro rear sight	11d	22
Rear sight elevation screw	11d(2)	22
Rear sight windage screw	11d(3)	22
Safety catch	11a	20
Cal 38 Special, Smith and Wesson revolver K-38 (masterpiece):		
Cylinder and yoke	12d	25
Extractor rod	12b	24
Hammer	12c	24
Rear sight elevation screw	12g	26
Rear sight windage screw	12h	26
Safety device	12e	25
Thumb piece	12a	24
Trigger	12f	26
Cal 30-06 Winchester rifle Model 70 (special match grade):		
Bolt handle	15a	28
Bolt stop	15b	28
Magazine	15c	28
Magazine cover catch	15d	28
Safety lock	16e	28
Trigger	15f	80
Lyman rear sight No. 48WH:		
Description	16a	80
Elevation knob	16b	380
Elevation scale	16c	80
Elevation scale pointer	16d	80

AGO 10003A

	Paragraph	Page
Controls and instruments-Continued		
Lyman rear sight No. 48WH-Continued		
Rear sight aperture disk	16g	30
Windage knob	16e	31
Windage scale	16f	31
Lyman target front sight No. 77:		
Description	17a	31
Inserts	17b	31
Removal and installation	17c	31
Data plates	4	12
Data, tabulated	5	15
Description (See specific items),		
Disassembly (See specific items)		
During storage, inspection	95c	91
Failure to fire:		
Cook-off	42a (3)	49
Hangfire	42a (2)	49
Misfire	42a(1)	49
Procedures for removing a cartridge.	42b	49
Field report of accidents	2c	3
Field stripping (See specific items)		
Final inspection	90, 91	89
Firing (See specific item)		
Forms	2	3
Frame group (cal..22 high-standard automatic pistol (supermatic)):		
Assembly	63d	67
Description	63a	65
Disassembly	63b	65
Maintenance	63c	67
Grip frame group (cal..22 Ruger Mark I automatic pistol (target model)):		
Assembly	69d	71
Description	69a	69
Disassembly	69b	69
Maintenance	69c	69
Guard bow group:		
Assembly	87d	86
Description	87a	86
Disassembly	87b	86
Maintenance	87e	86
Hot-weather conditions	29	39
Installation (See specific items)		
Lubrication (See specific items)		
Lyman front sight No. 48WH:		
Assembly	85d	85
Disassembly	85b	84
Maintenance	85c	84
Removal	85a	84
Lyman front sight No. 77:		
Assembly	84e	84
Disassembly	84a	82
Maintenance	84b	84

	Paragraph	Page
Lyman rear sight No. 525, receiver extension rear sight:		
Assembly	88e	87
Description	88a	87
Disassembly	88c	87
Maintenance	88a, d	87
Magazine assembly (cal..22 high-standard automatic pistol (supermatic)):		
Assembly	62d	65
Description	62a	65
Disassembly	62b	65
Maintenance	62c	65
Magazine assembly (cal..22 rifle M12 Winchester rifle, Model 52 (heavy barrel)).	75	75
Magazine assembly (cal..22 Ruger Mark I automatic pistol (target model)):		
Assembly	68d	69
Description	68a	69
Disassembly	68b	69
Maintenance	68e	69
Mainspring housing assembly (cal..22 Ruger Mark I automatic pistol (target model)).	66	68
Maintenance (See specific items)		
Malfunctions of weapons (table III)	43	50
Moist or salty atmosphere	31	40
Name plates	4	12
Operation under unusual conditions:		
Cold-weather conditions	28	39
General	27	39
Hot-weather conditions	29	39
Moist or salty atmosphere	31	40
Sandy or dusty conditions	30	40
Operation under usual conditions (See specific items)		
Parts:		
Maintenance	54	59
Spare	33	41
Preventive-maintenance services (table II).	37-40	45-47
Procedures for removing a cartridge	42b	49
Receiver group:		
Assembly	86d	86
Description	86a	86
Disassembly	86b	86
Maintenance	86c	86
Records	2	3
Redfield olympic target front sight assembly.	89	89
Reports	2	3
Sandy or dusty conditions	30	40
Service upon receipt of materiel:		
General	6	17
New materiel	7	17

AGO 10003A

	Paragraph	Page
Service upon receipt of materiel-Continued		
Used materiel	8	17
Shipment and storage:		
Army shipping documents	95*b*	91
Limited storage instructions	96	91
Preparation for shipment	95*c*	91
Responsibility	95*a*	91
Slide assembly (cal..22 high-standard automatic pistol (supermatic)):		
Assembly	61*d*	63
Description	61*a*	63
Disassembly	61*b*	63
Maintenance	61*c*	63
Stock assembly (cal 30-06 Winchester rifle Model 70 (special match grade)).	82	82
Spare parts	33	41
Stock group (cal..22 rifle M12 (Remington rifle Model 40X-S1)):		
Assembly	80	82
Disassembly	80*a*	81
Maintenance	80*b*	81
Tables:		
Authorized cartridges (table V)	--	90
Preventive-maintenance services (table II).	--	48
Special tools and equipment for operation and preventive maintenance (table I).	--	41

	Paragraph	Page
Tables-Continued		
Troubleshooting (table III)	--	50
Troubleshooting (table IV)	--	61
Tabulated data	5	15
Target zeroing	26	38
Tools and equipment:		
Common:		
Maintenance	55	59
Preventive maintenance	34	41
Special:		
Maintenance	56	59
Preventive maintenance (table I).	35	41
Trigger housing assembly (cal..22 rifle M12 (Remington rifle Model 40X-S1)):		
Assembly	79*c*	81
Disassembly	79*b*	81
Removal	79*a*	81
Troubleshooting:		
Maintenance instructions	58	61
Preventive maintenance	41-43	49, 50
Unloading (See specific items)		
Unsatisfactory equipment or materials, report of.	2*d*	4
Unusual conditions	27-31	39, 40
Zeroing, target	26	38

AGO 10003A

[AG 474.6 (9 Apr 59)]

BY ORDER OF THE SECRETARIES OF THE ARMY AND THE AIR FORCE:

L. L. LEMNITZER,
General, United States Army,
Chief of Staff.

OFFICIAL:
R. V. LEE,
Major General, United States Army,
The Adjutant General.

THOMAS D. WHITE,
Chief of Staff, United States Air Force.

OFFICIAL:
J. L. TARR,
Colonel, United States Air Force,
Director of Administrative Services.

Distribution:
  Active Army:
    CNGB (1)
    ASA (2)
    Tech Stf, DA (1) except
      CofOrd (14)
    Ord Bd (2)
    USCONARC (3)
    US ARADCOM (2)
    US ARADCOM Rgn (2)
    USCINCEUR (5)
    OS Maj Comd (2)
    OS Base Comd (2)
    Log Comd (3)
    MDW (1)
    Armies (3) except
      First USA (5)
    Corps (2)
    Div (2)
    Brig (2)
    Regt/Gp/bg (1) except
      Ord Gp (2) except
        TOE 9-22 (none)
    Bn (1) except
      Ord Bn (2) except
        TOE 9-45, 9-375 (none)
    Ord Co (2) except
      TOE 9-12, 9-17, 9-46, 9-47,
      9-57, 9-229, 9-347, 9-367,
      9-376, 9-377 (none)
    Fld Comd, Def Atomic Spt
      Agcy (1)
    Ft Bragg (2)
    Ft Hood (7)
    Ft Bliss (9)
    Ft Sam Houston (7)
    Ft Sill (6)
    Svc Colleges (2)
    Br Svc Sch (2) except
      USA Ord Sch (50)
    PMST Sr Div Ord Units (1)
    Ord Ammo Comd (1)
    GENDEP (2)
    Ord Sec, GENDEP (5)
    Ord Dep (10) except
      Rossford Ord Dep (12)
      Anniston Ord Dep (18)
    Ports of Emb (OS) (2)
    Trans Terminal Comd (2)
    Army Terminals (2)
    OS Sup Agcy (1)
    Ord PG (10)
    Ord Arsenals (5) except
      Raritan Arsenal (33)
      Frankford Arsenal (30)
      Benicia Arsenal (20)
    Mil Dist (1)
    USA Corps (Res) (1)
    Sector Comd, USA Corps (Res) (1)
    Ord Proc Dist (1)
    MAAG (1)
    Mil Msn (1)
    JBUSMC (2)
    JUSMAG, Greece (2)
    Units org under fol TOE:
      29-2 (2)

NG: State AG (3); units-same as Active Army except allowance is one copy to each unit.
USAR: None.
For explanation of abbreviations used, see AR 320-50.

AGO 10003A

U.S. GOVERNMENT PRINTING OFFICE : 1993 0 - 342-421 (80241)

RECOMMENDED CHANGES TO EQUIPMENT TECHNICAL PUBLICATIONS

SOMETHING WRONG WITH THIS PUBLICATION?

THEN... JOT DOWN THE DOPE ABOUT IT ON THIS FORM, CAREFULLY TEAR IT OUT, FOLD IT AND DROP IT IN THE MAIL!

FROM: (PRINT YOUR UNIT'S COMPLETE ADDRESS)

DATE SENT

PUBLICATION NUMBER	PUBLICATION DATE	PUBLICATION TITLE

BE EXACT... PIN-POINT WHERE IT IS	IN THIS SPACE TELL WHAT IS WRONG AND WHAT SHOULD BE DONE ABOUT IT:
PAGE NO	PARA-GRAPH	FIGURE NO	TABLE NO	

PRINTED NAME, GRADE OR TITLE, AND TELEPHONE NUMBER | SIGN HERE:

DA FORM 2028-2
1 JUL 79

PREVIOUS EDITIONS ARE OBSOLETE.

P.S.—IF YOUR OUTFIT WANTS TO KNOW ABOUT YOUR RECOMMENDATION MAKE A CARBON COPY OF THIS AND GIVE IT TO YOUR HEADQUARTERS.

TEAR ALONG PERFORATED LINE

PIN: 026384-000